Microsoft® Excel for Accounting

AUDITING AND ACCOUNTING INFORMATION SYSTEMS

Katherine T. Smith, D.B.A.
Business Consultant

L. Murphy Smith, D.B.A., CPA
Texas A&M University

Lawrence C. Smith, Jr., Ph.D.
Louisiana Tech University

Pearson Education

UPPER SADDLE RIVER, NEW JERSEY 07458

Acquisitions Editor: Alana Bradley
Editor-in-Chief: P. J. Boardman
Editorial Assistant: Jane Avery
Program Consultant: Walter Mendez
Executive Marketing Manager: Beth Toland
Managing Editor (Production): John Roberts
Permissions Coordinator: Suzanne Grappi
Associate Director, Manufacturing: Vincent Scelta
Production Manager: Arnold Vila
Manufacturing Buyer: Michelle Klein
Cover Design: Kiwi Design
Printer/Binder: Victor Graphics

Pearson Education LTD.
Pearson Education Australia PTY, Limited
Pearson Education Singapore, Pte. Ltd
Pearson Education North Asia Ltd
Pearson Education, Canada, Ltd
Pearson Educación de Mexico, S.A. de C.V.
Pearson Education–Japan
Pearson Education Malaysia, Pte. Ltd

10 9 8 7 6 5 4 3 2
ISBN 0-13-008552-9

DEDICATION

To the students who use this book. We hope each of you will enjoy the true success which is measured by moral character and personal integrity. Solomon said, "A good name is more desirable than great riches; to be esteemed is better than silver or gold."

To our beloved children: Jacob, Tracy, and Hannah. "Children are a gift from God; they are His reward" (Psalm 127:3). You are treasures from heaven.

To our parents: Genita and Hubert Taken, and Doris and Junior Smith.

KTS & LMS

To Doris Elaine Barfoot Smith, my beautiful wife. To Chris, Snook, Patti, Doug, and Angie. You've blessed my life.

LCS

CONTENTS

PREFACE

The purpose of this book is to introduce students to the fundamental tools and techniques available in Microsoft Excel™ spreadsheet software. Applications are presented that pertain to specific auditing and AIS topics. Students will learn through experience by following directions and creating the example worksheets shown in each chapter. Assignments may be selected from those contained within the book or other sources provided by your instructor.

The book provides detailed instructions for using Microsoft Excel. These instructions are designed for the most current version of Excel but are applicable for most other versions as well. Additional information is available on the website corresponding to this book.

WEBSITE

For updates, example files, suggested assignment schedules, and other helpful information, check the website (http://www.IOLBV.com/murphy/EXCEL4AcctAA).

ACKNOWLEDGMENTS

The authors are grateful for the contributions to this project made by Michelle Chandler, Alana Bradley, and Kristi Shuey. We are thankful to Chris Osborne for regular doses of spiritual inspiration. Additionally, the authors appreciate the support and encouragement they have received, over the years, from the following colleagues:

Craig Bain, Northern Arizona University
Alan Blankley, University of North Carolina at Charlotte
James Flagg, Texas A&M University
Danny Ivancevich, University of North Carolina at Wilmington
Susan Ivancevich, University of North Carolina at Wilmington
David Kerr, Texas A&M University
Jeff Miller, Augusta State University
Steve McDuffie, Southwest Missouri State University
Uday Murthy, Texas A&M University
Alan Sangster, University of Aberdeen
Bob Strawser, Texas A&M University
Jim Thompson, Oklahoma City University
Chris Wolfe, Texas A&M University

About the Authors

Katherine Taken Smith

Dr. Katherine T. Smith has served on the faculties at the University of Mississippi and Louisiana Tech University. Dr. Smith has authored numerous research articles which have appeared in various professional journals such as *The CPA Journal, Today's CPA, Accounting Education* (UK), and *National Public Accountant*. Currently she serves on the editorial boards of five national journals. She has authored seven books, including an educational novel entitled *The Bottom Line is Betrayal* (http://www.iolbv.com/murphy/novels/) which has been described as an "instructional thriller" that provides an innovative way to present business concepts and issues to students. In addition, she has made presentations at professional meetings in the U.S. and abroad.

L. Murphy Smith

Dr. L. Murphy Smith, CPA is Assistant Department Head and Professor in the Accounting Department at Texas A&M University. He received his doctorate from Louisiana Tech University. Dr. Smith's accomplishments include numerous professional journal articles, research grants, books, and professional meeting presentations in the U.S. and abroad. His major research interests are systems, auditing, ethics, and international issues. His work has been cited in various news media, including *Fortune, USA Today*, and *The Wall Street Journal*. Among the books he has published, his accounting information systems text (http://acct.tamu.edu/smith/books/aisbook/) is now in its third edition. He serves on the editorial boards of several journals, including *Advances in International Accounting, Journal of Information Systems, Research on Accounting Ethics, Teaching Business Ethics*, and *The CPA Journal*.

Lawrence C. Smith, Jr.

Lawrence C. Smith, Jr., PhD is a Professor of Economics at Louisiana Tech University. He received his doctorate from the University of Mississippi. He has developed expertise on a wide variety of business and economics issues. In his distinguished career, Dr. Smith has made significant academic contributions in teaching, research, and service. He has played many roles in various professional organizations, including serving 27 years as Secretary-Treasurer of the Academy of Economics and Finance. In 1999 he was selected as the first Fellow of the Academy of Economics and Finance.

Dr. Smith's accomplishments include numerous professional journal articles, books, and professional meeting presentations. Among the journals in which he has published are the following: *Journal of Economic Education, Journal of Economics and Finance, Southwestern Economic Review, Journal of Real Estate Appraisal and Economics*, and *Oil, Gas & Energy Quarterly*.

Computer Basics 1

This chapter briefly describes components of the personal computer, operating systems software, Windows, and starting your spreadsheet program.

COMPONENTS OF THE COMPUTER

As shown in Exhibit 1.1, the basic personal computer system consists of a monitor, keyboard, and a central processing unit (CPU). The CPU consists of three components: main memory, arithmetic logic unit, and supervisory control. Main memory includes random access memory (RAM) and read-only memory (ROM). The RAM of a typical personal computer may be as little as 640 kilobytes (K) or as much as 256 megabytes (MB).

The box or chassis containing the CPU also contains other devices such as the graphics card which connects to the monitor, a parallel port which connects to a printer, a serial port which connects to a mouse, a modem which connects to the phone line, a hard disk drive which provides secondary storage (typically ranging from four to 100 gigabytes), a floppy disk drive, and a CD-ROM or CD-RW drive. Another increasingly common feature on personal computers is a network card (e.g. ethernet) which enables a computer to be connected to a local area network or intranet, which then permits access to the Internet and the World Wide Web. The most widely used floppy disk drive is the 3.5 inch high density (HD) drive. The 3.5 inch HD disk can store 1.44 megabytes (MB) of data. A CD-ROM or CD-RW can store up to 640 MB of data.

The keyboard on your computer is made up of three basic sections: the function keys, the numeric key pad, and the alphanumeric keys. The alphanumeric keys, the main part of the keyboard, include letters, numbers, and a variety of symbols. The function keys, labeled F1 through F12, have different uses depending on the software currently in use.

The numeric pad is located on the right side of your keyboard. A significant key on the numeric pad is the NUM LOCK key, which is a toggle key that enables the user to switch between the number keys and the cursor control keys located on the numeric pad.

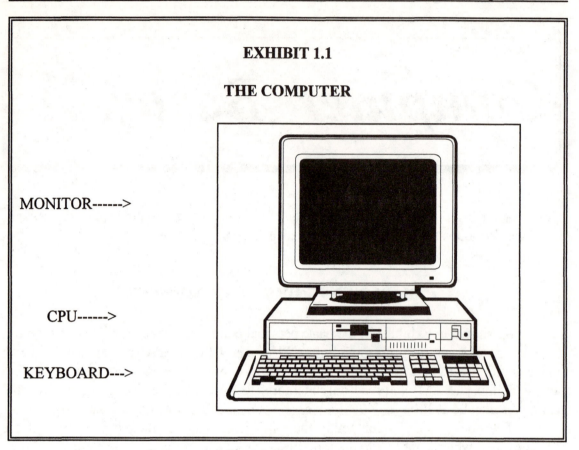

EXHIBIT 1.1

THE COMPUTER

MONITOR------>

CPU------>

KEYBOARD--->

OPERATING SYSTEMS SOFTWARE

An operating system runs your computer and manages your computer's activities. The operating system of the personal computer functions much like the operating systems on the mainframe or minicomputer. For the IBM-compatible system, the most popular operating system is Microsoft's Windows. The Apple Macintosh has an operating system called System 7.

Windows is a set of software programs that provides a graphical user interface. When running Windows, the computer user interacts with the computer visually and by use of a mouse rather than typing commands. New versions of Windows are typically released with much fanfare. Windows XP was introduced in New York City to a backdrop of a gospel choir singing "America the Beautiful," followed by pop star Sting performing a free concert in Bryant Park.

WINDOWS OPERATING SYSTEM

The most prominent feature of Windows is the use of icons (little pictures) to represent programs or groups of programs. After Windows is loaded (running), you run programs such as Excel by moving the pointer to the icon and double-clicking the left mouse button. A program icon represents a "shortcut" in Windows. Programs can also be accessed via the "start" button on the lower menu-bar. By clicking on "Start," you are given various options such as Run, Find, Settings, and Programs.

Microsoft periodically upgrades its Windows program. The current release is Windows XP. In Windows, "folders" and "shortcuts" refer to directories and executable programs. A folder may contain several shortcuts (which access specific programs such as Excel or Lotus 1-2-3). Each folder has a menu bar which allows creation of shortcuts or folders within that folder (select "File"-"New").

LOADING YOUR EXCEL SPREADSHEET PROGRAM

Excel by Microsoft Corporation is the most widely used spreadsheet software. To start Excel, follow these steps:

1. In Windows, use your mouse to click on the "Start" button on the bottom left side of your computer screen. The button should expand into a box with several options for selection.

2. From the Start menu, select the Programs options, which will open another box with options. If Microsoft Excel is listed separately, double-click the Excel option to open (run) the program. If there is not a separate listing for Microsoft Excel, then scroll to the Microsoft Office option and select Microsoft Excel.

OR

* If an Excel icon is shown on the screen, double-click on that icon.

BASIC COMMANDS

SAVING A FILE

A worksheet is saved like any other file by using the following commands:

1. Choose "File" in the menu bar and select the Save-As option.
2. The Save-As menu box will appear and the name "Book1.xls" will be highlighted in the file name box. "Book1" is simply the default name which Excel uses and "xls" is the filename extension of an Excel worksheet. You can replace "Book1" with a new filename; we recommend keeping the "xls" extension so that your file will be recognized as an Excel worksheet.
3. Now that you have named the worksheet, you can save it in the future by simply clicking on the Save icon (picture of a floppy disk).

CLOSING FILES

Similar to other files, a worksheet is closed by simply clicking on the "X" button in the upper right-hand corner of the menu bar on your worksheet.

RETRIEVING FILES

A worksheet is retrieved like any file by using the following commands:

1. Click on the "Open" icon (picture of an open folder).
2. An Open File box will appear with a list of files or folders. Double-click on the file you want opened. Note: If the file is not listed, then you are in the wrong folder. Access the correct folder by clicking on the arrow next to the "Looking in" box at the top. A list of folders or directories will appear for your choosing. Alternatively, you can search for a file with Windows Explorer program (using "Tools - Find").

EXITING

The Excel program can be exited like any other program by clicking on the "X" button in the upper right-hand corner of the screen (this appears above the "X" button used for closing the worksheet).

Making a Worksheet 2

WORKSHEET LAYOUT

Once the spreadsheet software is loaded, a screen appears similar to Exhibit 2.1. A spreadsheet file is often referred to as a worksheet.

EXHIBIT 2.1
BASIC EXCEL WORKSHEET

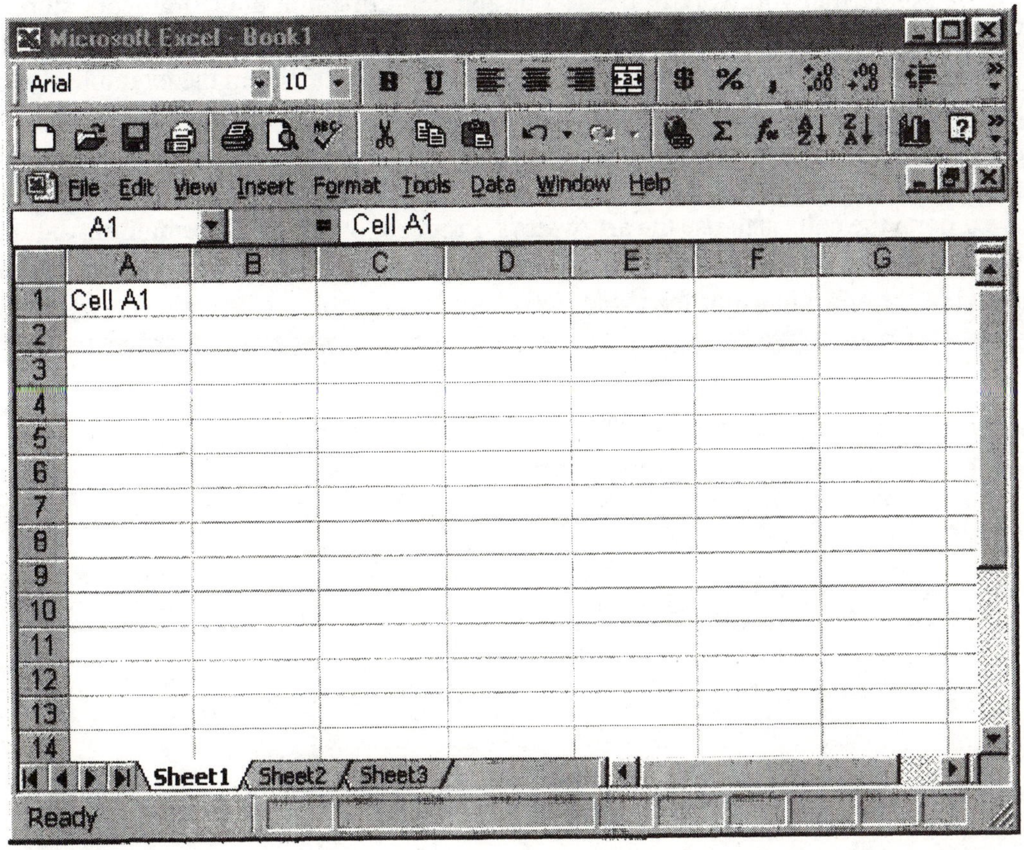

The letters across the top of a worksheet correspond to columns. The numbers along the left side of a worksheet correspond to rows. The box at the intersection of a column and row is referred to as the cell location. Cells are where data, either text or mathematical expressions, are entered. In Exhibit 2.1, the words "Cell A1" have been typed into cell A1. Directly above the cell is the control panel which shows the cell designation, in this case it is A1. To the right of that, next to an equal sign, you'll notice another panel containing "Cell A1." When a cell is clicked upon, its contents automatically appear in this panel.

Each Excel file, called a workbook, can hold several worksheets. Worksheets are saved, closed and printed like any other file, by clicking on the "File" selection in the top menu bar or by clicking on the appropriate icons.

AN ILLUSTRATION

To begin your familiarization with Excel worksheets, we will create a worksheet using just the essential commands. Step-by-step instructions to accomplish these commands will be provided.

Assume that you work in the accounting department at a local grocery store. Your boss has requested a breakdown of sales by department, comparing the last two years. To accomplish this, we'll create a worksheet with the data contained in the example worksheet shown in Exhibit 2.2. To begin, click on cell A1 with your mouse and type in "Sales." When finished typing, press Enter or click on another cell; the typed data will automatically be inserted into the worksheet. Now click on cell A3 and type in "Produce." Another way to move among the cells is to use the arrow keys. Proceed to type in the remaining data so that your worksheet looks like Exhibit 2.2. Column B is left empty simply for the purpose of improving the appearance of the worksheet.

EXHIBIT 2.2
GROCERY STORE WORKSHEET

	A	B	C	D	E
1	Sales				
2			12/31/x1	12/31/x2	
3	Produce		300	350	
4	Bakery		100	150	
5	Florist		50	20	
6	Deli		225	290	
7	Meat		550	600	
8	Dairy		410	500	
9					
10					

Note that Excel automatically right-justifies a number after it is entered into a cell. If you make a mistake in typing the numbers, the ensuing section on editing will reveal how to correct it.

EDITING

A cell can be put into edit mode by double clicking on the cell. Excel will then allow you to move around within the cell and change the contents. If you want to replace the entire contents of a cell, simply click on the cell once and type in the new contents. If you want to delete the entire contents of a cell, click on the cell and press the delete key.

As noted earlier, when a cell is clicked upon, its contents automatically enter the panel at the top of the worksheet next to the equal sign (=). Another way to edit a cell is to place your cursor within this panel and type.

If you make a mistake using any of the following commands, you can undo it by clicking on the "undo" icon (an arrow curving backwards).

MOVING CELL CONTENTS

Perhaps our worksheet would look better if "Sales" was placed more in the center of the worksheet. To move "Sales" to cell C1:

1. Click on the cell you wish to move (A1).
2. Position your cursor anywhere along the border of the cell until the cursor turns into a white arrow. Hold down the left mouse button and drag the arrow to the new cell. Release the mouse button, and the contents will appear in the new cell.

To move a block of cells, highlight the cells by holding down the left mouse button and then move the entire block at once. Cells can also be moved by using the "copy and paste" commands (discussed later in the chapter).

INSERTING ROWS AND COLUMNS

Suppose you decide that the worksheet would look better with a space between the title and the date headings. You want to insert a blank row between "Sales" on row 1 and the dates on row 2. The row can be inserted as follows:

1. Rows are added **above** the cell pointer, so position your cell pointer accordingly. In our example, click on any cell in row 2.
2. Click on "Insert" in the menu bar and choose "Rows" to insert.

Suppose you want to insert a column between the years (columns C and D). Columns are added to the **left** of the pointer, so to add the column in our example, click on any cell in column D. Click on "Insert" in the menu bar and choose "Columns." Exhibit 2.3 shows the new format with a blank row 2 and the sales figures in columns C and E.

EXHIBIT 2.3
GROCERY STORE WORKSHEET

	A	B	C	D	E
1			Sales		
2					
3			12/31/x1		12/31/x2
4	Produce		300		350
5	Bakery		100		150
6	Florist		50		20
7	Deli		225		290
8	Meat		550		600
9	Dairy		410		500
10					
11					

DELETING AND SHIFTING CELLS

Assume that the Florist department was discontinued at our store last month and should not be in the worksheet. As previously discussed, the contents of a cell can be removed by clicking on the cell and pressing the delete key. However, we want the florist data removed without leaving a row of empty cells. This is accomplished by deleting the unwanted row and shifting the remaining rows up. Regarding our grocery store worksheet, use the following commands:

1.   Click on the cell which contains "Florist."
2.   Click on "Edit" in the menu bar and choose the Delete option.
3.   Excel gives you the option of deleting the entire row; click on that option. The rows below the deleted row will be shifted up.

If we had not chosen the option of deleting the entire row, than only the cell containing "florist" would have been deleted and only the cells within column A would have been shifted up. If an entire column is deleted, columns will be shifted to the left.

CENTERING

Data within a single cell can be centered by clicking on the cell and then clicking on the icon which displays centered lines. The icon is found on the top toolbar, just to the right of the bold (**B**), italicize (*I*), and underline (<u>U</u>) icons. Center each of the dates in the worksheet. Multiple cells may be centered at the same time by first highlighting the range of cells and then clicking on the icon.

Suppose we need a different heading on the worksheet. Delete "Sales." In the same cell, type "Grocery Store Sales by Department." The heading will run over into the adjacent empty cells. Press enter to leave the edit mode. To center the new heading between columns A and E, first highlight row 1 from A to E. Then click on the icon with the boxed-in "a" (merge and center icon) at the top of the tool bar. Exhibit 2.4 shows the new heading.

CHANGING COLUMN OR ROW WIDTH

When the spreadsheet program is first loaded, the column width will be eight characters. If your cell data exceeds the cell width, the data will simply run into the adjacent empty cell. However, if the adjacent cell is not empty, the overflow data will be truncated at the cell border. To avoid this, column width can be changed. Using our example worksheet, type the heading "Total Sales Per Year" into cell A9. To accommodate the long heading, widen column A using the following instructions. Note: It is best to be out of the edit mode when changing cell width; click on a blank cell to exit the edit mode.

1. Position the cursor at the top of the screen on the mid-point between the lettered column headings (i.e., between A and B). The cursor should change into a "+."
2. Click-and-drag using the left mouse key; hold it while "dragging" the column to a different width.

Your worksheet should now resemble Exhibit 2.4. (We will total the sales per year in Chapter 3 using a special Excel command.) Row width can be changed by positioning the cursor between the row numbers on the left side of the worksheet.

COPY AND PASTE

The "copy and paste" commands enable you to duplicate the contents of one or more cells to other locations on the worksheet. Anything already in the receiving cell will be deleted. To copy and paste, highlight the cell(s) to be copied, click on the copy icon, then move the cursor to the desired location and click the paste icon. If you want to delete the cell contents from the original location, you can use the cut and paste icons or the commands which are accessed via "Edit" on the menu bar.

EXHIBIT 2.4
GROCERY STORE WORKSHEET

	A	B	C	D	E
1	Grocery Store Sales by Department				
2					
3			12/31/x1		12/31/x2
4	Produce		300		350
5	Bakery		100		150
6	Deli		225		290
7	Meat		550		600
8	Dairy		410		500
9	Total Sales Per Year				
10					
11					

Special paste commands can be accessed by clicking on "Edit" in the menu bar and choosing the "Paste Special" option. Here are two useful "paste special" commands which can be used on cells or entire worksheets.

1. The "Microsoft Excel Worksheet" option allows you to paste a worksheet into a document (e.g. a Word file) and then activate Excel by simply clicking on the worksheet in your document.

2. The "Picture" option pastes the worksheet contents without the gridlines. The grocery store worksheet was pasted into Exhibit 2.5 using the Picture option.

EXHIBIT 2.5
WORKSHEET PASTED USING "PICTURE" OPTION

Grocery Store Sales by Department

	12/31/x1	12/31/x2
Produce	300	350
Bakery	100	150
Deli	225	290
Meat	550	600
Dairy	410	500
Total Sales Per Year		

PRINTING

For printing your worksheet, it is helpful to first highlight the section you want printed and then click on "File" in the menu bar. Select "Print." Under the print options, choose "Selection." Another very useful step is to select "File - Print Preview" to see how your output will look. By skipping these steps, and depending on where the cursor is, you could print several pages unnecessarily. Occasionally, you may need to designate the range of cells to be printed. To do so, highlight the range to be printed (e.g. A1 to H40) and then click on File - Print Area - Set Print Area.

Formulas, Functions, and Formatting   *3*

This chapter presents Excel features which are especially useful for manipulating numbers within accounting related worksheets. The features include automatic sums, formulas, functions, and numeric formatting.

The Grocery Store worksheet that was created in Chapter 2 will also be used in this chapter as an example. If you do not still have the worksheet on your computer, recreate it as shown in Exhibit 3.1

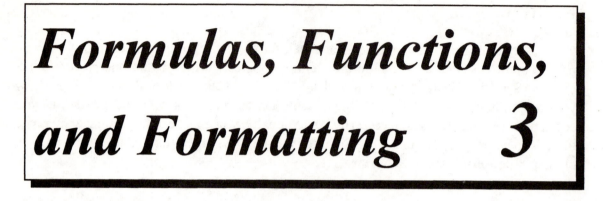

EXHIBIT 3.1
GROCERY STORE WORKSHEET

	A	B	C	D	E
1	Grocery Store Sales by Department				
2					
3			12/31/x1		12/31/x2
4	Bakery		100		150
5	Deli		225		290
6	Produce		300		350
7	Dairy		410		500
8	Meat		550		600
9	Total Sales Per Year				
10					

AUTOMATIC SUMS

Excel contains an icon with the Greek sigma sign (Σ). This icon is called "Autosum" and will automatically sum numbers within the cells you select. Using the example worksheet, total each year's sales using the following instructions:

1.   Highlight the cells to be summed (for year 1: cells C4 through C8).

2.   Click on the Autosum button. The total will automatically be inserted into the next lower cell (C9).

In the latest version of Excel, the Autosum icon is accompanied by a down arrow. Upon clicking on the arrow, other functions will be displayed, such as averaging numbers and counting cells.

Note: If a number has more characters than a cell will hold, the number signs (####) will appear. To correct this, simply widen the column or decrease the font size.

Repeat the Autosum process for the second year's column. To enhance the appearance of the worksheet, place a line under the figures being summed (i.e., cells C8 and E8). To place an underscore in a cell, click on the appropriate cell and then click on the underscore icon (U). Your worksheet should now resemble Exhibit 3.2.

EXHIBIT 3.2
GROCERY STORE WORKSHEET

	A	B	C	D	E
1	Grocery Store Sales by Department				
2					
3			12/31/x1		12/31/x2
4	Bakery		100		150
5	Deli		225		290
6	Produce		300		350
7	Dairy		410		500
8	Meat		550		600
9	Total Sales Per Year		1585		1890

FORMULAS

WRITING FORMULAS

Formulas can be used to manipulate numeric data. They are entered just as they would be processed algebraically. For example, to add the contents of cells C9 and E9, the following steps are necessary:

1.   In the cell in which you want the result to appear, type the formula: =C9+E9

2.   Press "Enter" to place the results of the equation in the cell.

The same process applies to subtraction, division, and multiplication. The multiplication symbol is the asterisk (*). The division symbol is the slash (/).

Note: When an equal sign is the very first thing entered, Excel knows it is a mathematical expression. If there is a space before the equal sign, Excel will read it as text.

COPYING FORMULAS

We will use our grocery store worksheet to practice writing and copying formulas. Suppose the boss wants a column which shows how much sales have increased or decreased between the two years. Type the heading "Difference" into cell D3. Next, in cell D4, type the formula: =E4-C4. Press "Enter."

Instead of entering the formula into multiple cells, you can copy this formula into the other cells. The cell addresses will automatically adjust as you copy a formula from one cell to another. If a formula is copied down the length of a column, the address will change corresponding to the row in which the formula is placed. Copy the formula into the other cells in your worksheet by:

1.   Click on the cell which contains the formula (D4). Put the cursor on the small box in the bottom right corner of the cell (the fill handle); the cursor will turn to a "+".
2.   Drag the cell over the range of cells you want to fill (D5 through D9).

When the formula was copied into cell D5, the formula automatically changed from "=E4-C4" to "=E5-C5." This is referred to as **relative addressing**. Relative addressing occurs for both rows and columns.

Your worksheet should now resemble Exhibit 3.3. In the newest version of Excel, an Autofill options box pops up; it can be ignored. Autofill will be discussed in Chapter 5.

The alternative to relative addressing is called **absolute addressing**. This means that the cell references do not adjust, but they remain exactly as they were in the source cell of the copy procedure. To make a formula absolute you must precede that portion of the formula with a dollar sign ($). Thus, if you want to copy a formula such as =C2*D5 and you want to make C2 an absolute address, you would type the formula as =C2*D5 before copying.

EXHIBIT 3.3
GROCERY STORE WORKSHEET

	A	B	C	D	E
1	Grocery Store Sales by Department				
2					
3			12/31/x1	Difference	12/31/x2
4	Bakery		100	50	150
5	Deli		225	65	290
6	Produce		300	50	350
7	Dairy		410	90	500
8	Meat		550	50	600
9	Total Sales Per Year		1585	305	1890
10					

FUNCTIONS

Functions are basically pre-written formulas. They save time and increase accuracy. We will create a new worksheet to practice using functions. Remember that a workbook can contain several worksheets. If you want to add a new worksheet to an existing workbook file, simply click on the tab at the bottom entitled "Sheet2." If you prefer an new workbook file, one can be created by clicking on the icon of a blank white sheet of paper found on the upper-left of the tool bar.

Assume that you are asked to prepare a worksheet to calculate loan payments based on the information below. Type the data from Exhibit 3.4 into a new worksheet. Note that column A will need to be widened to accommodate the words "annual payments." Review: To widen a column, position the cursor on the mid-point between the lettered column headings. When the cursor changes into a "+," click-and-drag the column width.

EXHIBIT 3.4
LOAN PAYMENTS WORKSHEET

	A	B	C	D
1	Rate	0.1	0.05	0.06
2	Years	10	20	8
3	Principal	100000	30000	20000
4	Annual Payments			

To calculate the annual payments for our example loan payments worksheet, the use of the @PMT function is explained below.

1. Click on the cell in which you want the annual payment to appear (B4).
2. Click on the "fx" icon which represents the Functions Wizard.
3. Choose Financial under the Functions category box.
4. Choose PMT under the Function name box. Then click OK.
5. Enter the cell locations which contain the rate, nper, and pv. Use the mouse to click on the different boxes.
   In this example, rate is B1. Nper (years) is B2. Pv (principal) is B3. (The formula is =PMT(rate, nper, pv). Excel will also ask for fv and type; leave those blank. Click on OK.

Note: If a cell is not wide enough to accommodate a number, then you will see "######" in the cell. Simply widen the column and the correct number ($16,274.54) will appear. Excel automatically formats the loan payment in dollars.

Do not use the Functions Wizard to calculate the remaining annual payments; instead we will save time by copying the formula into the other cells. Review on how to copy a formula: Click on the cell which contains the formula (B4). Put the cursor on the small box in the bottom right corner of the cell; the cursor will turn to a "+". Drag the cell over the range of cells you want to fill (C4 and D4).

Exhibit 3.5 includes the annual loan payment calculations.

EXHIBIT 3.5
LOAN PAYMENTS WORKSHEET

	A	B	C	D
1	Rate	0.1	0.05	0.06
2	Years	10	20	8
3	Principal	100000	30000	20000
4	Annual Payment	($16,274.54)	($2,407.28)	($3,220.72)

DATE AND OTHER FUNCTIONS

The Functions Wizard of Excel has many useful functions available in addition to those that perform basic arithmetic. For example, by typing "=today( )" into a cell, the worksheet will always show the actual date. If you typed a particular date into the parentheses, the worksheet would always show that date. Other functions and their symbols are described in Exhibit 3.6.

EXHIBIT 3.6
EXCEL FUNCTIONS

SYMBOL   DESCRIPTION

Financial Functions:

FV	Returns the future value of an investment.
IPMT	Returns the interest payment for an investment for a given period.
IRR	Returns the internal rate of return for a series of cash flows.
NPV	Returns the net present value of an investment based on a series of periodic cash flows and a discount rate.
PMT	Returns period payments for an annuity.
PV	Returns the present value of an investment.
RATE	Returns the interest rate per period of an annuity.

Date and Time Functions:

DATE	Returns the serial number of a particular date.
DAY	Converts a serial number to a particular day of the month.
DAYS360	Calculates the number of days between two dates based on a 360-day year.
TIMEVALUE	Converts the time in the form of text to a serial number.
TODAY	Returns the serial number of today's date.

Math and Trig Functions:

COUNTIF	Returns the number of nonblank cells in a given range which meet the given criteria.
INT	Rounds a number down to the nearest integer.
ROUND	Rounds a number to the specified number of digits.
SUBTOTAL	Returns a subtotal in a list or database.
SUM	Adds the specified numbers.

Statistical Functions:

AVERAGE	Returns the average of the specified numbers
COUNT	Counts how many numbers are in a given range.
MAX	Returns the maximum number in a specified range.
MEDIAN	Returns the median of the specified numbers.
MIN	Returns the minimum number in a specified range.
MODE	Returns the most common value in a specified range.

NUMERIC FORMATTING

Using our example loans payment worksheet, we will format the numbers in a simple manner using the tool bar icons. Customized formatting using the menu bar will also be discussed.

PERCENTAGE SYMBOL

The icon of a percentage symbol (%) automatically converts numbers to percentages. In your worksheet, select the cells which contain values for Rate (B1 through D1) and click on the percentage icon. If your software doesn't have the percentage icon, click on "Format - Cells" in the menu bar and then select "Number - Percentage." Exhibit 3.7 shows the percentages.

CURRENCY STYLE

The icon of a dollar sign ($) is called "currency style" and will automatically add a dollar sign, decimal, and cents places to any cell you select. In your worksheet, select the cells which contain values for Principal and click on the dollar icon. Alternatively, click on "Format - Cells" in the top menu bar and then select "Number - Currency."

If you accidentally insert a currency style into the wrong cell, you must go to the Format menu to un-format the cell. Click on "Format" in the menu bar and choose "Cells." Under the Number tab choose "Currency." Excel will offer several options, scroll till you select "None" for symbols and "0" for the number of decimal places. Variations in currency formats are described in the Customized Formatting section.

Your worksheet should now resemble Exhibit 3.7.

EXHIBIT 3.7
LOAN PAYMENTS WORKSHEET

	A	B	C	D
1	Rate	10%	5%	6%
2	Years	10	20	8
3	Principal	$ 100,000.00	$ 30,000.00	$ 20,000.00
4	Annual Payment	($16,274.54)	($2,407.28)	($3,220.72)

COMMAS

The icon of a comma automatically inserts commas into the appropriate places. The columns will automatically widen to accommodate the numerical formatting.

CUSTOMIZED FORMATTING

If you need a format other than what the icons provide, you can customize the formatting of a cell through the menu bar by using the following instructions.

1. Highlight the cells to be formatted.
2. Click on Format in the menu bar and select "Cells."
3. Choose the category and options you desire.

Exhibit 3.8 displays some of the variations in numeric formatting.

EXHIBIT 3.8
EXAMPLES OF AVAILABLE NUMERIC FORMATS

Format Type	Display
Number	1234 1,234.00 (any number of decimal places may be chosen) -1,234.56 (negative number can also be in parenthesis or in red)
Date	3/14 3/14/98 March - 98 March 14, 1998 3/14/98 1:30 PM Some options have the time displayed along with the date.
Time	13:30 1:30 PM 13:30:55
Percentage	5% or 5.00% (any number of decimal places may be chosen)
Currency	$1,234 $1,234.00 (any number of decimal places may be chosen) $(1,234.56) negative number
Special	Numbers can be formatted as zip codes, phone numbers, or social security numbers.

Charts 4

The spreadsheet program allows you to create charts or graphs as a way to visually represent numeric data. Excel refers to both charts and graphs as simply "charts." Before creating a chart, the data which is to be used in the chart must be typed into a worksheet. Next, you highlight the data and click on the Chart Wizard icon (a bar chart with blue, yellow, and red columns). The Chart Wizard will guide you through a four step process for creating a chart. A chart is linked to the worksheet data and is automatically updated when the data in the worksheet is changed. The following sections give specific directions on creating different types of charts.

First, set up a new worksheet containing the data in Exhibit 4.1; this data will be used for each of the following charts. Assume that you work for a company which has sales in the United States, Europe, and Asia.

EXHIBIT 4.1
SALES WORKSHEET

	A	B	C	D	E	F
1	SALES BY YEAR AND BY REGION					
2						
3		USA	Europe	Asia	Total Sales	
4	2002	534	231	69		
5	2001	518	146	71		
6	2000	427	75	44		
7	1999	405	239	22		
8	1998	267	119	36		
9	1997	188	84	25		
10						

Use the Autosum icon to total the sales for each year. Review: Highlight the row containing the first year's sales (cells B4 through D4). Click on Autosum and the total will automatically be entered into the next cell (E4). Remember to save time by copying the formula (cell E4) into the remaining cells (cells E5 to E9). Review: Click on the cell which contains the formula (E4). Put the cursor on the small box in the bottom right corner of the cell; the cursor will turn to a "+". Drag the cell over the range of cells you want to fill.

In the latest version of Excel, a green triangle may appear which indicates that a message corresponds to that cell. In this case, Excel is notifying us that the formula did not sum all of the cells in the row (we intentionally did not include the cell containing the year).

COLUMN CHART

A column chart, like a line chart, is a one-dimensional chart. Assume your boss wants to see a comparison of each region's sales over the past six years. You decide to use a column chart. First, highlight the data range which contains the information that will be plotted, in this case that would be the columns containing the years and each region's sales, including their titles (i.e., cells A3 through D9). The headings are being included so that Chart Wizard can use them in the chart legend. Next, click on the Chart Wizard icon. It will present the following four steps:

Step 1. Select a specific chart type. For this example, select Column chart. Then you will be able to choose from several chart sub-types. Choose the first sub-type box which is labeled "clustered column." Click on "Next."

Step 2. In this step, Chart Wizard is confirming the data range which you previously highlighted and the fact that your data is in columns. There is a display showing what your chart currently looks like. Click on "Next."
Note: By default, Chart Wizard plots whatever there is fewer of - rows or columns - as the data series. Since our example has fewer columns, the columns containing sales figures were automatically plotted as data series. Chart Wizard uses the first column as the x-axis IF it does not have a heading AND the remaining columns do. Thus, the column containing the years was automatically used for the x-axis instead of being plotted as another data series.

Step 3. Several chart enhancing options are made available here. Type a title into the title box. Type "Year" into the x-axis box and "Sales" into the y-axis box. These are the only selections necessary for this example. Click on "Next."

Step 4. Chart Wizard places the chart into your current worksheet unless you select the option of placing it into a new sheet. Click "Finish" and your chart will appear on your worksheet.

When completed, your column chart should resemble Exhibit 4.2. The chart can be repositioned on the worksheet by clicking on it and dragging it to a new position. The chart box can be enlarged by clicking and expanding its borders like any other box.

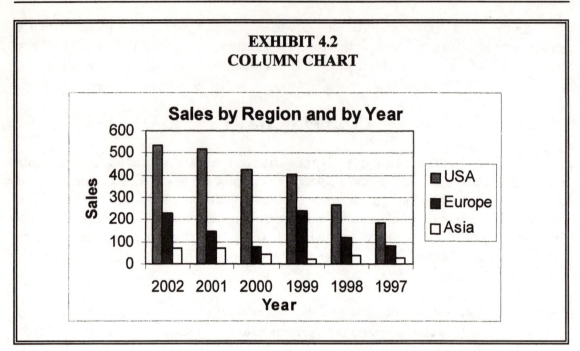

EXHIBIT 4.2
COLUMN CHART

To print a chart, highlight it and select "Print" or "Print-preview." Print-preview allows you to first make setup changes such as size and page orientation (portrait or landscape). To delete a chart from your worksheet, simply click on the chart and press the Delete key.

STACKED-COLUMN CHART

A stacked-column chart is one variation of a column chart. Instead of placing bars next to each other, it stacks shaded bars for multiple ranges of data on top of each other. Try charting the same data range using the stacked-column chart. Click on the Chart Wizard icon and follow the four step process previously described. After selecting the column chart type, we chose the second chart sub-type labeled "stacked column." Your chart should resemble the stacked-column chart in Exhibit 4.3.

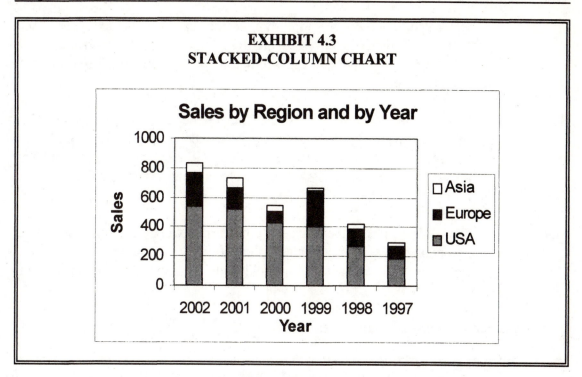

EXHIBIT 4.3
STACKED-COLUMN CHART

Sales by Region and by Year

LINE CHART

A line chart is used for plotting data on a vertical y-axis and a horizontal x-axis. The y-axis can contain from one to six ranges, producing one to six lines.

Suppose the boss wants to see the total sales trend over the past six years. You decide to use a line chart. The same four step process using Chart Wizard will be used, but this time we will describe some additional options. Highlighting the data range needed for the chart is a bit more difficult since the Total Sales column is not lined up next to the years in the worksheet. We could move the columns around on the worksheet, but instead we will select the x-axis values through the Chart Wizard process. First, highlight the Total Sales column (cells E3 through E9). Next, click on Chart Wizard.

Step 1.   Select the Line chart option. For the sub-type, we chose the first box in the second row which is labeled "Line with markers displayed." Click on "Next."

Step 2.   Chart Wizard is confirming our data range. There is a tab titled "Series," click on that tab. You'll see that Total Sales is listed as a data series. (If we had not highlighted the heading, it simply would be labeled Series 1. You could rename the data series at this point by typing a name into the "Name" box.)

At the bottom of the menu box, you'll see that the x-axis has not been designated. Click on the empty box beside "category (X) axis labels" and then, while still in Chart Wizard, highlight the years on your worksheet (cells A4 to A9). The range address will automatically be inserted into the box. Click on "Next."

Step 3.   Type in a chart title and axis labels. Click on the tab at the top marked "Data Labels." You are given options as to how to label the plotted line(s). Click on the option "show value." The sales values will appear on your chart. Chart Wizard will automatically show a chart legend unless you turn the option off in this step. Click on "Next."

Step 4.   Chart Wizard places the chart into your current worksheet unless you select the option of placing it into a new sheet. If you choose a new sheet, you can access the different sheets by clicking on the tabs at the bottom of the worksheet.

Exhibit 4.4 contains the line chart just created.

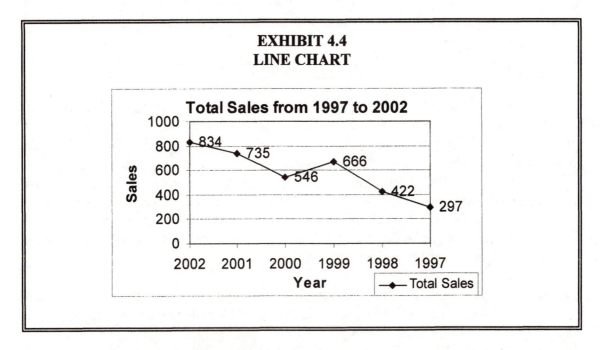

EXHIBIT 4.4
LINE CHART

Total Sales from 1997 to 2002

After you have created the chart, changes can be made to the style of its various parts by right-clicking on the specific part and choosing to re-format. For example, the following changes were made to the chart in Exhibit 4.4.

•   The background area of the chart was changed to white by right-clicking on the chart area and accessing the Format Plot Area menu box. Several colors and border styles are made available.

- The style of the plotted lines can be modified by right clicking on the line and accessing the Format Data Series. The style and color of the line can then be changed.

- Excel automatically positions the category labels (Years) between the tick marks on the x-axis and thus plots the values between the tick marks. You can change this and create a direct alignment by right-clicking on the category axis (x-axis) and bringing up the Format Axis menu box, as shown in Exhibit 4.5. Next, click on the "Scale" tab and un-check the box next to "Value (Y) axis crosses between categories."

EXHIBIT 4.5
FORMAT AXIS MENU BOX - SCALE TAB

Format Axis [?][X]

| Patterns | Scale | Font | Number | Alignment |

Category (X) axis scale

Value (Y) axis crosses
  at category number: [1]

Number of categories
  between tick-mark labels: [2]

Number of categories
  between tick marks: [1]

☐ Value (Y) axis crosses between categories
☐ Categories in reverse order
☐ Value (Y) axis crosses at maximum category

[OK] [Cancel]

PIE CHART

A pie chart can be used to graph only a single range of data (i.e., one column or one row of values). For this example, we'll chart the sales for the year 2002 only. First, highlight the **row** containing the 2002 sales data, and include the row containing the regional titles (cells B3 through D4). Click on Chart Wizard and follow the four step process. Under pie chart, we selected the second sub-type choice labeled "pie with a 3-D visual effect." In step 3, we chose to use percentages and names as data labels for the pie slices. We deleted the legend box.

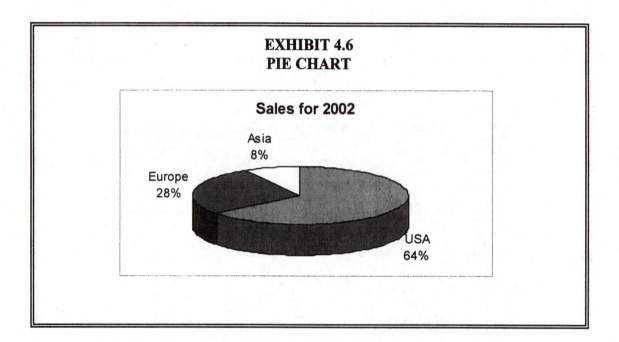

EXHIBIT 4.6
PIE CHART

Worksheet Manipulation 5

RANGE NAMES

Sometimes keeping track of the cell addresses to be included in a range can be quite tedious. Excel provides a command to name ranges and thus refer to the cell addresses by that name. Using range names is useful in sorting, formatting, copying, and printing.

We'll use the sales worksheet from Chapter 4 to practice creating a range name. The worksheet is shown in Exhibit 5.1. Suppose you frequently print the USA's sales figures and, thus, it would save time to use a range name instead of always highlighting the cells.

EXHIBIT 5.1
SALES WORKSHEET

	A	B	C	D	E
1	SALES BY YEAR AND BY REGION				
2					
3		USA	Europe	Asia	Total Sales
4	2002	534	231	69	834
5	2001	518	146	71	735
6	2000	427	75	44	546
7	1999	405	239	22	666
8	1998	267	119	36	422
9	1997	188	84	25	297

Create a range name for the USA column by following these steps:

1.   Highlight the cells that you want to name as a range (B3 through B9). (Note: If you include the title when you initially highlight the range,

Excel will automatically insert the title as the range name.)

2.   Click on "Insert" in the menu bar and select the Name option. Then select "Define."

3.   The name you selected will appear, or you can type in a new name. Click on "OK."

Click on a blank cell to remove the highlighting. Now click on the arrow within the cell designation panel (the box directly above column A). As shown in Exhibit 5.2, this will reveal any ranges which have been named. Click on the "USA" range name which you just created; this causes the USA column to be highlighted. Once a range name has been created, you may use this name anywhere that requires a cell address.

EXHIBIT 5.2
CELL DESIGNATION PANEL

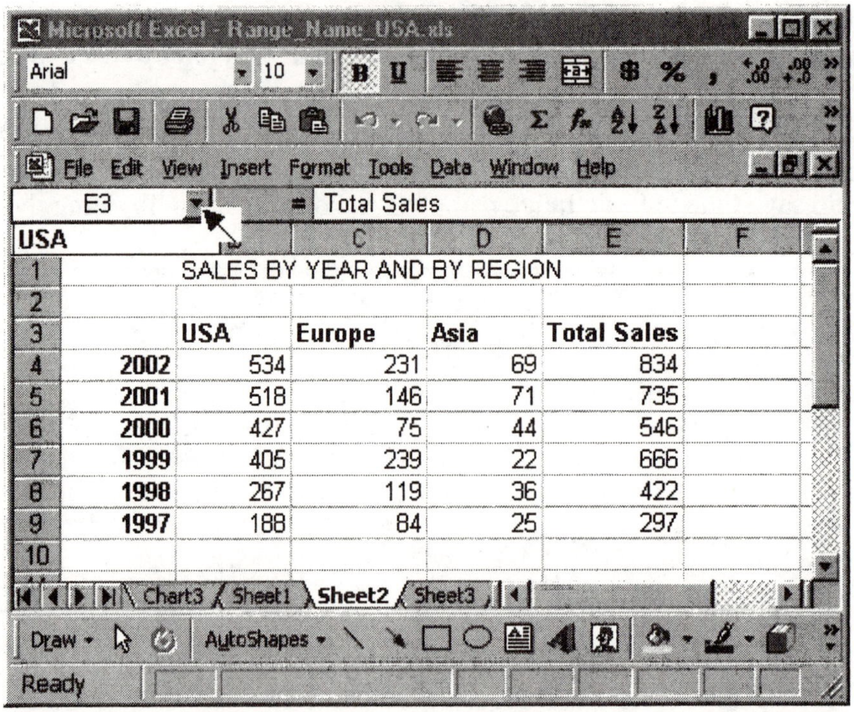

FREEZE PANES

When working on a large worksheet, sometimes the entire worksheet does not fit on the screen. The Freeze Panes command allows you to freeze rows or columns. The cells on one side of the freeze line remain stationary, while the cells on the other side of the line can be scrolled. For example, a row of headings can be frozen while you scroll and view the remainder of the worksheet. Exhibit 5.3 illustrates freezing row 3 of our example worksheet; note that row 3 has remained at the top of the display, while the remaining worksheet has been scrolled to row 9.

EXHIBIT 5.3
FREEZE PANES

	A	B	C	D	E	F
1		SALES BY YEAR AND REGION				
2						
3		USA	Europe	Asia	Total Sales	
9	1997	188	84	25	297	
10						

The Freeze Panes command allows you to compare any rows or columns of data which are not already adjacent on the worksheet.

To use the Freeze Panes option, perform the following steps:

1. Click on the cell where you want the freeze to be. (For our example, A4.)
   a. For a **horizontal** freeze, the rows **above** the cell will be frozen. Click on the first cell of the row.
   b. For a **vertical** freeze, the columns to the **left** of the cell will be frozen. Click on the first cell of the column.
2. Click on "Window" in the menu bar and select the Freeze Panes option.

If you do not click on the first cell in the row or column, then you will achieve horizontal and vertical splits simultaneously. To remove the freeze, click on "Window" and select the Unfreeze Panes option.

SPLIT SCREEN

Under "Window" in the menu bar, there is an option called "Split." This is very similar to freezing panes. The only difference is that the part of the worksheet chosen to remain constant can also be duplicated on the screen by scrolling past it. (The freeze panes option does not duplicate the constant part of the worksheet.) To create a split screen, follow the directions for freeze panes except chose "Split" instead of "Freeze Panes."

IMPORTING DATA

Using the Clipboard feature, you are able to copy or "import" data from other spreadsheets or programs into your Microsoft Excel worksheet.

1.   Open the file which contains the data you want imported into your Excel worksheet. Highlight the data that you want copied and copy it to the Clipboard by clicking on the copy icon (2 sheets of paper).

2.   Select the area on the Excel worksheet to where the information should be imported and click on the Paste icon (clipboard).

Database Tools 6

Excel has several features which improve the ease of manipulating data in a worksheet. This chapter specifically covers data form, data sort, Autofill, and Autofilter.

Excel provides a database function which allows you to assimilate and manipulate related information. A **database** consists of **records** which contain **fields.** Fields are items such as an account title, an account number, or amount. Fields are made up of alphabetic characters (e.g. account title) or numbers (e.g. amount). Fields that are related are grouped together in records. For example, an accounts receivable record typically includes a field for account number, customer name, and balance. All the accounts receivable records comprise the database (customarily referred to as the accounts receivable master file).

Prepare a new worksheet with the data contained in Exhibit 6.1 using the following Excel feature called "data form."

DATA FORM

The purpose of data form is to reduce errors resulting from entering data into the wrong cell. When using data form, you provide Excel with the titles you want on the worksheet and it inserts these titles into a simplified form. You can then add information record by record. To duplicate the example worksheet using data form, perform the following steps:

1.   Type the titles (i.e., account, name, balance, past due) into your worksheet. Refer to Exhibit 6.1 for the exact placement.
2.   Highlight the titles. Click on "Data" in the menu bar and choose the "Form" option. You will be asked if the top row of your selection is the header row. Click on "OK."
3.   The form will automatically appear with your titles as the field names on the form. You can now begin entering data from your records. IMPORTANT: Use the TAB key when moving from one field to the next. After inserting all the data for one person (a record), press the Enter key.

Notes: Column B will need to be widened to accommodate the names. At this time, leave the "Account" field blank. When all the records are entered, click on Close. When you are finished, your worksheet should resemble Exhibit 6.1.

EXHIBIT 6.1
EXAMPLE ACCOUNTS WORKSHEET

	A	B	C	D	E
1	Account	Name	Balance	Past Due	
2		Miller, Rob	600	80	
3		Smith, John	220	20	
4		Jackson, Al	50	10	
5		King, James	200	60	
6		Brown, Amy	100	90	
7		Jones, Sara	145	40	
8					

DATA SORT

SORTING A SINGLE COLUMN OR ROW

Excel will sort numbers or words in an ascending or descending manner. The "sort ascending" icon displays the letter A on top of the letter Z; it will sort a list going from A to Z. The "sort descending" icon displays the letter Z on top of the letter A. A column can be sorted by simply clicking on any cell within the column and then clicking on the sort icon. Excel will prioritize alphabetic sorting over numeric sorting.

SORTING MULTIPLE COLUMNS OR ROWS

Suppose the boss wants to view the accounts receivable past due from shortest time past due to longest time past due. In this case, multiple columns need to be sorted in order to keep each person's record intact. Sorting is a bit more entailed since we want to sort by a specific column of numbers (past due amounts). Using your example worksheet, perform the following steps:

1. Highlight each record (i.e., cells B2 through D7).
2. Click on Data in the menu bar and choose "sort." Select the column by which you want the list sorted (past due). Excel gives you the option to sort ascending or descending; choose ascending.

Exhibit 6.2 shows the records by past due values in ascending order.

EXHIBIT 6.2
EXAMPLE ACCOUNTS WORKSHEET

	A	B	C	D
1	Account	Name	Balance	Past Due
2		Jackson, Al	50	10
3		Smith, John	220	20
4		Jones, Sara	145	40
5		King, James	200	60
6		Miller, Rob	600	80
7		Brown, Amy	100	90
8				

Now we will sort the worksheet in a different way using the data sort icon. Suppose the boss wants the list of names alphabetized in the worksheet. Again, to keep each person's record intact, multiple columns need to be sorted. Since Excel will prioritize alphabetic sorting over numeric sorting, it will automatically sort by the Names column (we do not need to specify a column). To alphabetize the records, performing the following steps:

1. Highlight the appropriate cells (B2 through D7).
2. Click on the "sort ascending" icon (picture of the letter A on top of the letter Z, with a down arrow along side of it).

Exhibit 6.3 shows the records alphabetized in ascending order.

EXHIBIT 6.3
RESULTS OF DATA SORT

	A	B	C	D
1	Account	Name	Balance	Past Due
2		Brown, Amy	100	90
3		Jackson, Al	50	10
4		Jones, Sara	145	40
5		King, James	200	60
6		Miller, Rob	600	80
7		Smith, John	220	20
8				

AUTOFILL

This command enables the user to fill a specified range with a sequence of numbers or text. Suppose you want to create a consecutive numbering system for customer account numbers, beginning with account number 1001 up to account number 1006. Perform the following steps:

1. Type the first two values of the series (i.e., 1001, 1002) into the first two cells of your list. (Refer to Exhibit 6.4.)
2. Highlight the two cells. Put the cursor on the small box in the bottom right corner of the cell (the fill handle); the cursor will turn to a "+".
3. Drag the cell over the range of cells you want to fill. Release the mouse and AutoFill will automatically fill in the series of cells.

The result of this procedure is displayed in Exhibit 6.4.

EXHIBIT 6.4
RESULTS OF AUTOFILL

	A	B	C	D
1	Account	Name	Balance	Past Due
2	1001	Brown, Amy	100	90
3	1002	Jackson, Al	50	10
4	1003	Jones, Sara	145	40
5	1004	King, James	200	60
6	1005	Miller, Rob	600	80
7	1006	Smith, John	220	20
8				

AUTOFILTER

This command permits the user to select and view records in a database which meet a specific criterion set forth by the user. You determine your criteria by selecting what data from which fields you want to keep. For example, you may choose to view only those records for people who are 40 days or more past due. AutoFilter will allow you to do this by performing the following steps:

1. Highlight all of the records including the titles.

2. Click on "Data" in the menu bar. Choose the Filter option and then the AutoFilter.

3. Small boxes with down arrows will appear in each cell containing a field title. These drop boxes will list options when the arrow is clicked.

4. In order to view only those records that are 40 days or more past due, click on the down arrow in the Past Due cell. Several options will appear, choose the Custom option. (If you selected one of the numbers displayed, than only those records containing that number would be shown.)

5. In the Custom AutoFilter menu box, click on the arrow within the first box in order to view your options. Select the "is greater than or equal to" option. Then, click on the next box to the right and type in "40." Click the OK button.

Your worksheet should now display only those records that are 40 days or more past due, as shown in Exhibit 6.5. To delete the AutoFilter, once again click on Data, then Filter, and uncheck the AutoFilter option by clicking on it.

EXHIBIT 6.5
RESULTS OF AUTOFILTER

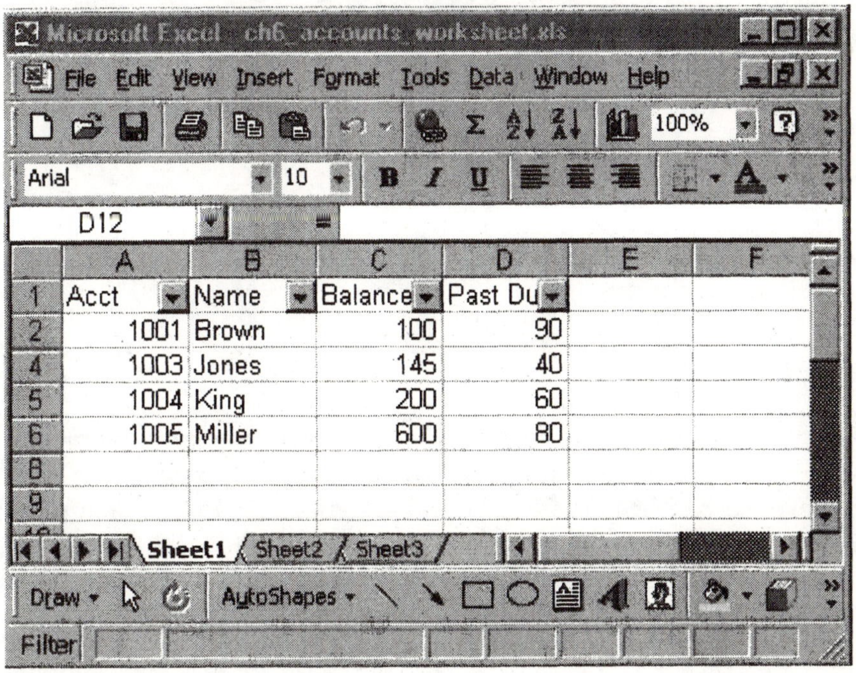

Macro Commands 7

Macros are shortcuts which allow you to reduce a series of different commands or keystrokes into a couple of simple clicks of the mouse. Microsoft Excel allows you to "record" the instruction of several commands and then replay or "run" the macro to activate the commands exactly as you performed them. Macros are efficient in performing time-consuming functions which are done frequently.

CREATING A MACRO

To illustrate the macro feature, we will use the example worksheet which was created in Chapter 6 and is shown below in Exhibit 7.1.

EXHIBIT 7.1
EXAMPLE ACCOUNTS WORKSHEET

	A	B	C	D
1	Account	Name	Balance	Past Due
2	1001	Brown, Amy	100	90
3	1002	Jackson, Al	50	10
4	1003	Jones, Sara	145	40
5	1004	King, James	200	60
6	1005	Miller, Rob	600	80
7	1006	Smith, John	220	20
8				

Suppose the boss wants the accounts sorted according to each person's balance, going from largest to smallest. Since the account balances change often, let's create a macro that runs the sort procedure. The following steps describe how to create a simple macro, in this case, for sorting a worksheet.

1.   Turn on the macro recorder by clicking on "Tools" in the menu bar

and choosing the Macro option and then "Record New Macro."

2.   Enter a name for your macro in the Name box. You may replace the name Excel automatically inserted (Macro1) with a name of your choosing, such as "Sort." Click on "OK."

3.   A small box will appear on your worksheet labeled "Stop." The macro program will record every action you perform from now until the time you press the blue button in the box.

4.   Perform the task you want done. In this case, perform the sort feature: Highlight all the records, but not the titles (i.e., highlight cells A2 to D7). If the box is in the way, it can be moved by clicking on the title and moving the cursor. Click on "Data" in the menu bar and choose "Sort." In the Sort box, select the Balance column in descending order. Click on "OK."

5.   Click on the blue button in the Stop box.

Your worksheet should now resemble Exhibit 7.2.

EXHIBIT 7.2
SORTED BY BALANCE USING A MACRO

	A	B	C	D
1	Account	Name	Balance	Past Due
2	1005	Miller, Rob	600	80
3	1006	Smith, John	220	20
4	1004	King, James	200	60
5	1003	Jones, Sara	145	40
6	1001	Brown, Amy	100	90
7	1002	Jackson, Al	50	10

RUNNING A MACRO

Let's make use of the macro we just created. Suppose the account balances have changed in the past week. John Smith reduced his balance down to $120 and James King reduced his balance down to $80. Insert these new figures into your worksheet. Now we'll resort the accounts using the macro. To run the macro, perform the following steps:

1.   Select "Tools" in the menu bar and choose the Macro option and then "Macros."

2.   Choose the macro program you want and click on "Run."

This sorting task was relatively simple, but it illustrates the potential that macros have in saving time on tasks that must be constantly repeated.

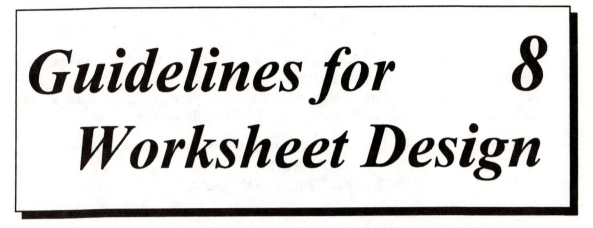

Guidelines for Worksheet Design   8

The following general guidelines should be considered when designing a worksheet; each will be discussed within this chapter.

1. Outline worksheet requirements (i.e., input and output).
2. Create a file identification area.
3. Establish data input areas separate from output areas.
4. Enter data in rows or columns, but not both.
5. Use manual recalculation when working with extremely large files.
6. Create backup files.
7. Test the worksheet.

REQUIREMENTS OUTLINE

The first guideline in creating a worksheet is to outline the worksheet requirements. What input is necessary to solve the problem at hand? What output is required? These requirements should be determined before beginning work. For example, assume you are required to create a worksheet that projects income statements for the next two years based on a constant growth rate in sales revenue. In this case, the required input is the current sales amount, annual sales growth rate, cost of goods sold as a percentage of sales, and the fixed amount of operating expenses.

The output requirement would be projected income statements for the next two years.

FILE ID

A file identification area should be prepared at the top of the worksheet. Prepare a new worksheet with the following file identification information: the file name, the worksheet designer's name, the input required, the output generated, and the dates the file was created, modified, and last used. See Exhibit 8.1 for an illustration.

EXHIBIT 8.1
FILE IDENTIFICATION AREA

	A	B	C	D	E
1	IDENTIFICATION AREA:				
2					
3	Filename: Forecast				
4	Designer:				
5	Input Required:				
6	a. Current sales amount				
7	b. Annual sales growth rate				
8	c. Cost of goods sold as a % of sales				
9	d. Operating Expenses				
10	Output: Projected Income Statements				
11	File Created:				
12	File Modified:				
13	Last Used:				
14					

DATA INPUT

The data items necessary for using the worksheet are typed into one column of the input area. For this example, cost of goods sold is assumed to be a constant percentage of sales and operating expenses are assumed to be a fixed amount each year. The input area for our example worksheet is illustrated in Exhibit 8.2. Enter these input items along with their respective values into your worksheet. Be sure to put the values into column E. (We will be inserting formulas later with the cell address of E.)

Formulas within the output area are based upon values in the input area. This enables the user to modify any value in the input area and instantly see how the change affects the output.

EXHIBIT 8.2
FILE ID AND INPUT AREA

	A	B	C	D	E
1	IDENTIFICATION AREA:				
2					
3	Filename:Forecast				
4	Designer:				
5	Input Required:				
6		a. Current sales amount			
7		b. Annual sales growth rate			
8		c. Cost of goods sold as a % of sales			
9		d. Operating Expenses			
10	Output: Projected Income Statements				
11	File Created:				
12	File Modified:				
13	Last Used:				
14					
15					
16	INPUT AREA:				
17					
18	Current sales ($):				1,000
19	Growth rate as a % of sales:				12%
20	Cost of goods sold as a % of sales:				60%
21	Operating expenses ($):				100
22					

DATA OUTPUT

The output area of the worksheet contains the desired results. The output for our example is projected income statements for the next two years. Exhibit 8.3 displays the output area items and formulas. Type these into your worksheet. For purposes of this example, the income statement is limited to only five line items. Exhibit 8.4 shows the computation results. Note: For uniformity, we formatted the income statements amounts to include two decimal places. This was easily accomplished by highlighting the appropriate cells and then clicking on the "increase decimal" icon (an arrow next to ".0"). Decimal places can also be specified by clicking on "Format" in the menu bar, as discussed in Chapter 3.

EXHIBIT 8.3
FILE ID, INPUT AND OUTPUT AREAS

	A	B	C	D	E
1	IDENTIFICATION AREA:				
2					
3	Filename:Forecast				
4	Designer:				
5	Input Required:				
6	a. Current sales amount				
7	b. Annual sales growth rate				
8	c. Cost of goods sold as a % of sales				
9	d. Operating Expenses				
10	Output: Projected Income Statements				
11	File Created:				
12	File Modified:				
13	Last Used:				
14					
15					
16	INPUT AREA:				
17					
18	Current sales ($):				1,000
19	Growth rate as a % of sales:				12%
20	Cost of goods sold as a % of sales:				60%
21	Operating expenses ($):				100
22					
23					
24	OUTPUT AREA:				
25					
26	Projected Income Statement for the Next Two Years				
27					
28				20x1	20x2
29					
30	Sales			=E18+E18*E19	=D30+D30*E19
31	Cost of goods sold			=D30*E20	=E30*E20
32					
33	Gross Profit			=D30-D31	=E30-E31
34	Operating Expenses			=E21	=E21
35					
36	Projected Net Income			=D33-D34	=E33-E34

EXHIBIT 8.4
OUTPUT AREA RESULTS

				20x1	20x2
24	OUTPUT AREA:				
25					
26	Projected Income Statement for the Next Two Years				
27					
28				20x1	20x2
29					
30	Sales			1120.00	1254.40
31	Cost of goods sold			672.00	752.64
32					
33	Gross Profit			448.00	501.76
34	Operating Expenses			100.00	100.00
35					
36	Projected Net Income			348.00	401.76

Once the output area is formatted by typing in the required items and formulas, the computations are totally formula driven, based upon values in the input area. As previously noted, this enables the user to modify any value in the input area and instantly see how the change affects the output. For example, change the growth rate percentage in the input area from 12% to 15%; you will instantly see the recalculations resulting in a net income of $360 for the first year and $429 for the second year.

INPUT ALIGNMENT

For maximum efficiency, the input cells should be aligned vertically (in a column) or horizontally (in a row), but not both. Fewer mistakes should occur if the user doesn't have to steer the cursor through a maze of input cells.

MANUAL RECALCULATION

If more than one value in the input area is to be changed on an extremely large worksheet, it is helpful to turn off Excel's automatic recalculation. This is because the software instantly recalculates mathematical expressions once a value has been modified. Data cannot be entered while the recalculations are taking place. The time involved is inconsequential for small worksheets but can become a burden for extremely large worksheets. A simple procedure is used to change from automatic recalculation to manual recalculation:

1. Click on "Tools" in the menu bar and choose "Options."
2. Select the Calculation tab.
3. In the Calculation area, click on "Manual."

In the Manual mode, when a value in the input area is changed, the output values will not change in response. If you wish for Excel to recalculate an amount, without reinstating the automatic recalculation option, you can press the F9 key. Excel will recalculate for the values currently in the worksheet. When using manual recalculation, a good idea is to type a note on the worksheet that you must press "F9" to recalculate.

BACKUP FILES

Backup copies should be continually updated and stored in more than one place. When creating a worksheet, the user should periodically (every 15 to 30 minutes) save the file in case of a power outage or other event that may cause erasure of the file and the loss of hours of work.

TESTING

Any new worksheet should be manually tested. If formulas are involved, the user must test the worksheet result against an example that is already proven correct.

Step-by-Step Excel Example 9

This chapter provides step-by-step instructions for creating a simple worksheet and graph using Microsoft Excel spreadsheet software.

CREATING AN EXCEL WORKSHEET

Open a new worksheet and enter the information shown in Exhibit 9.1. Brief reviews of some of the Excel features are given if you should need them. Note that the sales amount of 1000 dollars must be placed in cell C6.

EXHIBIT 9.1
EXAMPLE WORKSHEET

	A	B	C	D	E	F
1	IDENTIFICATION AREA:					
2	Filename: Example					
3	Designer:					
4						
5	INPUT AREA:					
6	Sales in $ =		1000			
7						
8	OUTPUT AREA:					
9	JACOB & SISTERS BRICK COMPANY					
10	INCOME STATEMENT					
11	For the Year Ended December 31, 20x1					
12						
13	Sales					
14	Cost of sales					
15	Gross profit					
16	Operating expense					
17	Net Income					
18						

EDITING A CELL

A cell can be put into edit mode by double clicking on the cell. Excel will then allow you to move around within the cell and change the contents. After you have finished the edit typing, press "Enter" to insert the contents into the worksheet. If you want to delete the entire contents of a cell, click on the cell and press the delete key.

CENTERING

After the company name and income statement headings are typed in, they are centered by highlighting each row individually from A to E (e.g. A9 to E9) and then clicking on the centering icon (the boxed-in letter "a" between arrows pointing left and right) at the top of the tool bar.

INSERTING FORMULAS

Formulas are entered just as they would be processed algebraically, using cell addresses to represent values in the equation. When an equal sign is the very first symbol entered, Excel knows this cell contains a mathematical expression. (If there is a space before the equal sign, Excel will read it as text.)

Assume that the company expects sales of $1,000 for the year ended 12/31/x1. The cost of sales is expected to be 60 percent of sales and operating expenses average 10 percent of sales. Using this information, we can create formulas for each of the items on our worksheet. Type the formulas from Exhibit 9.2 into your worksheet; press "Enter" after each entry.

EXHIBIT 9.2
FORMULAS FOR EXAMPLE WORKSHEET

	A	B	C	D	E
8	OUTPUT AREA:				
9		JACOB & SISTERS BRICK COMPANY			
10		INCOME STATEMENT			
11		For the Year Ended December 31, 20x1			
12					
13	Sales		=C6		
14	Cost of sales		=C13*.60		
15	Gross profit		=C13-C14		
16	Operating expense		=C13*.10		
17	Net Income		=C15-C16		

Your worksheet should now contain the correct values for each item, as shown in Exhibit 9.3

EXHIBIT 9.3
EXAMPLE WORKSHEET - OUTPUT

8	OUTPUT AREA:			
9	JACOB & SISTERS BRICK COMPANY			
10	INCOME STATEMENT			
11	For the Year Ended December 31, 20x1			
12				
13	Sales	1000		
14	Cost of sales	600		
15	Gross profit	400		
16	Operating expense	100		
17	Net Income	300		
18				

MANIPULATING DATA

The worksheet just created can be used for any amount of sales by simply changing the value for sales in the input area. The computations in the output area are totally formula driven, based on amounts in the input area. This enables the user to modify any value in the input area and instantly see how the change affects the output. For example, change the value of sales from $1000 to $2000 in the input area; click on cell C6 and type in 2000. You'll note that each item in the output area was automatically recalculated and the new net income is $600.

NUMERIC FORMATTING

If you wish to include dollar signs and commas, click on the cells containing currency. Once the cells are selected, click on the icon of a dollar sign ($). Alternatively, you can click on "Format" in the menu bar and then select "Cells - Number - Currency."

COLUMN EXPANSION

When the spreadsheet program is first loaded, the column width will be eight characters. If your cell data exceeds the cell width, the data will simply run into the adjacent empty cell; this is what occurred in our example worksheet. However, if the adjacent cell is not empty, the overflow data will be truncated at the cell border. To avoid this, column width can be changed using the following steps. Note: It is best to be out of the edit mode when changing cell width; click on a blank cell to exit the edit mode.

1.   Position the cursor at the top of the screen on the mid-point between the lettered column headings (i.e., between A and B). The cursor should change into a "+."

2.   Click-and-drag using the left mouse key; hold it while "dragging" the column to a different width.

PRINTING

For printing your worksheet, it is helpful to first highlight the section you want printed and then click on "File" in the menu bar. Select "Print." Under the print options, choose "Selection." Another very useful step is to select "File - Print Preview" to see how your output will look. By skipping these steps, and depending on where the cursor is, you could print several pages unnecessarily.

CREATING AN EXCEL PIE CHART

Before creating a chart, the data which is to be used in the chart must be typed into a worksheet. Next, you highlight the data and click on the Chart Wizard icon (picture of blue, yellow, and red columns on a bar chart). The Chart Wizard will guide you through a four step process for creating a chart. A chart is linked to the worksheet data it's created from and is automatically updated when the data in the worksheet is changed

We'll prepare a pie chart of the division of sales revenue using Chart Wizard. A pie chart can be used to graph only a single range of data (i.e., one column or one row of values). Use the values corresponding with sales of $2000. Skip down a couple of lines on your worksheet and type in the data as shown in Exhibit 9.4.

EXHIBIT 9.4
SCHEDULE OF DATA FOR PIE CHART

	A	B	C
20	Cost of sales		1200
21	Operating expense		200
22	Net Income		600

Highlight the data range which contains the information that will be charted (C20 to C22). Next, click on the Chart Wizard icon. It will present the following four steps:

Step 1.   Select a specific chart type. For this example, select Pie chart. Then you will be able to choose from several chart sub-types. Choose the first sub-type box which is labeled "Pie." Click on "Next."

Step 2.   In this step, Chart Wizard is confirming the data range which you previously highlighted and the fact that your data is in columns. There is a display showing what your chart currently looks like. There is a tab titled "Series," click on that tab. Here, we can insert labels for our pie slices. Click on the empty box next to "Category Labels" at the bottom. Then, while still in Chart Wizard, highlight the labels on your worksheet (cells A20 to A22 containing the words "cost of sales, operating expense, net income"). The range address will automatically be inserted into the box. Click on "Next."

Step 3.   Several chart enhancing options are made available here. Type a title into the title box. Under the Data Labels tab, we choose "show percent." Click on "Next."

Step 4.   Chart Wizard places the chart into your current worksheet unless you select the option of placing it into a new sheet. Click "Finish" and your chart will appear on your worksheet.

Your pie chart should resemble Exhibit 9.5. The chart can be repositioned on the worksheet by clicking on it and dragging it to a new position. The chart box can be enlarged by clicking and expanding its borders like any other box.

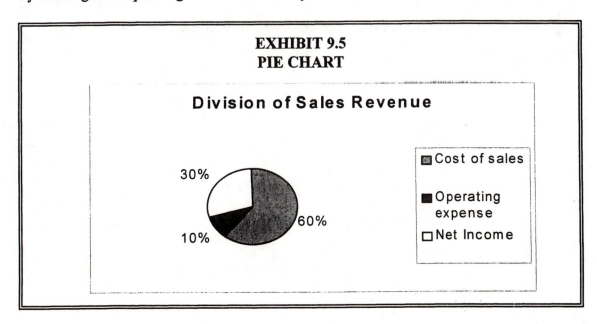

EXHIBIT 9.5
PIE CHART

Division of Sales Revenue

Spreadsheet Assignments
for
Auditing and AIS

LIST
of Spreadsheet Assignments

The list below provides a brief description of each assignment and related accounting topic area. Solutions to selected assignments are shown at the end of the book. In addition, a number of example worksheet files are available on the book's website (IOLBV.com/murphy/EXCEL4AcctAA).

ACCOUNTING TOPIC	No.	DESCRIPTION
Overview of The AIS and	1*	Income Statement
The Audit Environment	2	Cost of Goods Sold
	3	Financial Statements
Audit Risk Model	4	Detection Risk
	5	Detection Risk
Audit Planning and Decision Support	6	Financial Ratios
	7	Financial Ratios
	8	Common-Size Balance Sheets
	9	Common-Size Balance Sheets
	10	Horizontal Analysis of Income Statement
Internal Control and Computer Crime	11	Cash Budget
	12	Cash Budget
	13	Bank Reconciliation
	14	Cash Budget
	15	Bad Debt Expense
	16	Bad Debt Expense
	17	Aging Sales Invoices
	18	Aging Sales Invoices
	19	Aging Sales Invoices

---

* Indicates that the solution to the assignment is at the end of this book.

ACCOUNTING TOPIC	No.	DESCRIPTION
Auditing the AIS: Evaluating Internal Control	20	Attribute Sampling: Determining Sample Size
	21*	Attribute Sampling: Determining Sample Size
	22	Attribute Sampling: Evaluating Results
	23*	Attribute Sampling: Evaluating Results
	24	Attribute Sampling: Evaluating Results
Auditing the AIS: Evaluating Account Balances	25*	Variables Sampling: Determining Sample Size
	26	Variables Sampling: Determining Sample Size
	27	Variables Sampling: Determining Sample Size
	28	Variables Sampling: Evaluating Results
	29*	Variables Sampling: Evaluating Results
	30	Variables Sampling: Evaluating Results
Computer Controls	31	Product Mix Analysis
	32	Make or Buy Analysis
	33	Best Use of Facilities Analysis
Revenue Cycle	34	Sales by Product Type
	35*	Cost-Volume-Profit Analysis
	36	Cost-Volume-Profit Analysis
	37	Cost-Volume-Profit Analysis: Graph
	38	Cost-Volume-Profit Analysis: Graph
	39	Contribution Margin Income Statement
	40	Departmental Income Statement

* Indicates that the solution to the assignment is at the end of this book.

ACCOUNTING TOPIC	No.	DESCRIPTION
Expenditure/Distribution Cycle	41	Cash Disbursements
	42	Cost of Merchandise
	43	Cost of Merchandise
	44	Tracking Inventory Quantity
	45	Product Cost Schedule
	46	Perpetual Inventory Record
	47	Income Statement, Balance Sheet, and Statement of Cash Flows
Conversion Cycle	48	Cost Allocation Rates
	49*	Budgeted Costs: ABC Cost per Unit
	50	Manufacturing Cost Based on ABC Unit Cost
	51	Units-of-Production Depreciation
	52	Joint Cost Allocation
	53	Joint Cost Allocation
	54	Allocation of Costs in Lump-Sum Purchase
Financial Cycle	55	Statement of Owner's Equity
	56	Preparation of Adjusted Trial Balance
	57	Financial Statements and Related Questions
	58	Post-Closing Trial Balance
	59	Trial Balance and Worksheet
	60	Bond Amortization Schedule
International Issues	61*	Foreign Currency Translation Using the Current Rate Method
	62	Foreign Currency Translation Using the Current Rate Method
	63	Foreign Currency Translation Using the Current Rate Method
	64	Foreign Currency Translation Using the Current Rate Method

---

* Indicates that the solution to the assignment is at the end of this book.

1. INCOME STATEMENT

Create an Income Statement for Chris Ray's Card Shop for year ended 12/31/x1. See Chapter 9 for an example. Assume that sales are expected to be $100,000. The cost of sales is 50% of sales and operating expenses are 15% of sales. The income statement should include the following line items: sales, cost of sales, gross profit, operating expenses, and net income. Note: The solution to this problem is at the end of the book.

2. COST OF GOODS SOLD

Create the following cost of goods sold statement.

DORIS' DIAMOND CO.
COST OF GOODS SOLD
For Year Ended 12/31/x2

Beginning Inventory	$ 75,000
Purchases	25,000
Goods Available	$100,000
Ending Inventory	20,000
Cost of Goods Sold	$ 80,000

3. FINANCIAL STATEMENTS

Examine Exhibits A and B. Exhibit A summarizes the eleven transactions of Gary Lyon, CPA, for the month of April 20x1. Suppose Lyon has completed the first seven transactions only and needs a bank loan on April 21, 20x1. The vice president of the bank requires financial statements to support all loan requests.

Prepare the income statement, statement of owner's equity, and balance sheet that Gary Lyon would present to the banker after completing the first seven transactions on April 21, 20x1. Exhibit B shows the financial statements on April 30.

EXHIBIT A
Analysis of Transactions of Gary Lyon, CPA

	Cash	+	Accounts Receivable	+	Supplies	+	Land		
(1)	+ 50,000								
Bal.	50,000								
(2)	- 40,000						+40,000		
Bal.	10,000						40,000		
(3)					+500				
Bal.	10,000				500		40,000		
(4)	+ 5,500								
Bal.	15,500				500		40,000		
(5)			+3,000						
Bal.	15,500		3,000		500		40,000		
(6)	- 1,100								
	- 1,200								
	- 400								
Bal.	12,800		3,000		500		40,000		
(7)	- 400								
Bal.	12,400		3,000		500		40,000		
(8)	Not a transaction of the business								
(9)	+ 1,000		- 1,000						
Bal.	13,400		2,000		500		40,000		
(10)	+22,000						- 22,000		
Bal.	35,400		2,000		500		18,000		
(11)	- 2,100								
Bal.	33,300		2,000		500		18,000	=	53,800

Assets label: "Assets" appears above Cash/Accounts Receivable/Supplies/Land.

EXHIBIT A (cont.)

	Liabilities	+	Owner's Equity	Type of Owner's Equity Transaction
	Accounts Payable	+	Gary Lyon, Capital	
(1)			+ 50,000	*Owner investment*
Bal.			50,000	
(2)			————	
Bal.			50,000	
(3)	+ 500		————	
Bal	500		50,000	
(4)			+ 5,500	*Service revenue*
Bal.	500		55,500	
(5)	————		+ 3,000	*Service revenue*
Bal.	500		58,500	
(6)			- 1,100	*Rent expense*
			- 1,200	*Salary expense*
	————		- 400	*Utilities expense*
Bal.	500		55,800	
(7)	- 400			
Bal.	100		55,800	
(8)				
(9)	————		————	
Bal.	100		55,800	
(10)	————		————	
Bal.	100		55,800	
(11)	————		- 2,100	*Owner withdrawal*
	100		53,700	= 53,800

EXHIBIT B
Financial Statements of Gary Lyon, CPA

Gary Lyon, CPA
Income Statement
Month Ended April 30, 20x1

Revenue:
  Service revenue $8,500
Expense:
  Salary expense $1,200
  Rent expense   1,100
  Utilities   400
  Total expenses   2,700
Net income $5,800

Gary Lyon
Statement of Owner's Equity
Month Ended April 30, 20x1

Gary Lyon, capital, April 1, 20x1 . . . . $ 0
Add: Investments by owner   50,000
      Net income for the month   5,800
. . . .   55,800
Less: Withdrawals by owner . . . .   (2,100)
Gary Lyon, capital, April 30, 20x1 . . . . $53,700

Gary Lyon, CPA
Balance Sheet
April 30, 20x1

Assets		**Liabilities**	
Cash	$33,300	Accounts payable	$ 100
Accounts receivable	2,000		
Office supplies	500	**Owner's Equity**	
Land	18,000	Gary Lyon, capital	53,700
		Total liabilities and	
Total assets	$53,800	owner's equity	$53,800

Gary Lyon, CPA
Statement of Cash Flows*
Month Ended April 30, 20x1

Cash flows from **operating** activities:

  Receipts:
    Collections from customers ($5,500 + $1,000).. $ 6,500

  Payments:
    To suppliers ($1,100 + $400 + $400)................ $(1,900)
    To employees..   (1,200)   (3,100)
      Net cash inflow from operating activities........   3,400

Cash flows from **investing** activities:
  Acquisition of land... $(40,000)
  Sale of land..   22,000
    Net cash outflow from financing.....................   (18,000)

Cash flows from financing activities:
  Investment by owner... $ 50,000
  Withdrawal by owner...   (2,100)
    Net cash inflow from financing activities.......   47,900
Net increase in cash.. $33,300
Cash balance, April 1, 20x1...................................   0
Cash balance, April 30, 20x1................................. $33,300

*Refer to your textbook for more information regarding this statement.

---

4.   DETECTION RISK

Audit risk (AR) is the risk that the auditor renders the wrong opinion on the financial statements being audited. By definition, AR is the risk that the auditor fails to modify the opinion on financial statements that are materially misstated. AR is the product of three independent risks: 1) inherent risk (IR), 2) control risk (CR), and 3) detection risk (DR). IR is the risk that a material misstatement occurs in an account balance or class of transactions. CR is the risk that this misstatement is not prevented or detected by the auditee's internal control structure. DR is the risk that this misstatement is not detected by the auditor's substantive testing procedures. Assume that the auditor has set AR at 5 percent. Also, the auditor has set IR at 100 percent and, following the evaluation of the internal control structure, set CR at 20 percent. What will be the allowable DR?

5.   DETECTION RISK

Same as the prior assignment, except audit risk is set at 10 percent and control risk is set at 50 percent. What will be the allowable detection risk?

6.   FINANCIAL RATIOS

Use the following formulas to compute financial ratios for Junior's Computer Store for 20x4. The balance sheets and income statements for 20x4 and 20x3 are provided below. Design the worksheet so that the financial statements are in the input area and the financial ratios are in the output area.

FINANCIAL RATIOS

Liquidity Ratios:

Current Ratio =	(Cur. Assets)/(Cur. Liabilities)
Acid-Test Ratio =	(Cur. Assets - Inven. - Prepaid Exp.)/(Cur. Liabilities)

Activity Ratios:

Receivables Turnover =	(Net Credit Sales)/(Avg. A/R)
Inventory Turnover =	(Cost of Goods Sold)/(Avg. Inventory)
Asset Turnover =	(Net Sales)/(Avg. Assets)

Profitability Ratios:

Earnings Per Share =	(Net Inc. - Pref. Div.)/(Common Shares Outstanding)
Price to Earnings (P/E) =	(Market Price per Com. Share)/(EPS)
Dividend Payout =	(Div. per Com. Share)/(EPS)
Sales Profit Margin =	(Net Income)/(Net Sales)
Return on Assets =	(Net Income + Int. Exp. - Tax Savings from Int. Exp.)/(Avg. Assets)
Return on Com Stk Eq =	(Net Inc. - Pref. Div.)/(Avg. Com. Stk Equity)

Financial Stability Ratios:

Total Debt to Total Assets =	(Total Liabilities)/(Total Assets)
Times Interest Earned =	(Earnings before Int. and Taxes)/(Interest Charges)
Book Value Per Share =	(Com. Stk Equity)/(Com. Shares Outstanding)
Cash Flow Per Share =	(Net Inc + Noncash Charges)/(Com. Shares Outst.)

FINANCIAL STATEMENTS

Junior's Computer Store
Comparative Balance Sheets
12/31/x4 and 12/31/x3

	12/31/x4	12/31/x3
ASSETS:		
Cash	$1,200,000	$ 1,100,000
Accounts Receivable	780,000	550,000
Inventory	1,850,000	1,600,000
Fixed Assets (net)	8,200,000	7,200,000
Total Assets	$12,030,000	$10,450,000
LIABILITIES:		
Accounts Payable	$1,200,000	$900,000
Long-Term Debt	1,730,000	430,000
Total Liabilities	$2,930,000	$1,330,000
STOCKHOLDERS EQUITY:		
Preferred stock, $100 par, 12% cum	$1,800,000	$1,800,000
Common stock, $100 par	7,000,000	7,000,000
Retained Earnings	300,000	320,000
Total	$9,100,000	$9,120,000
Total Liabilities + Stockholders Equity	$12,030,000	$10,450,000
Market Price of Common Stock	$109	$107

Junior's Computer Store
Comparative Income Statements
FYE 12/31/x4 and 12/31/x3

	12/31/x4	12/31/x3
Sales	$4,000,000	$3,300,000
Cost of Goods Sold	2,200,000	1,650,000
Gross Profit	$1,800,000	$1,650,000
Operating Expenses:		
Depreciation	$738,000	$576,000
Advertising	45,000	38,000
Other	120,000	140,000
Total Operating Expense	$903,000	$754,000
Operating Income	$897,000	$896,000
Interest on Long-Term Debt	80,000	80,000
Income Before Taxes	$817,000	$816,000
Taxes	326,800	326,400
Net Income	$490,200	$489,600
Dividends Declared on Preferred Stock	$220,000	$220,000
Dividends on Common Stock	290,200	299,600
Net Income to Retained Earnings	($20,000)	($30,000)

NOTE: All sales are credit sales; the tax rate is 40%.

7.   FINANCIAL RATIOS

Same as the previous assignment but change the following 20x4 items:

A.	Accounts Receivable:	$780,000 to $1,780,000
B.	Accounts Payable:	$1,200,000 to $1,400,000
C.	Retained Earnings:	$300,000 to $1,100,000
D.	Sales:	$4,000,000 to $5,000,000

NOTE: The change in these financial statement items will affect other items.

8. COMMON-SIZE BALANCE SHEETS

Using the comparative balance sheets in Assignment 6, prepare common-size balance sheets. To prepare common-size balance sheets, divide all items by the "total assets" amount; thus, total assets each year (i.e., 20x4 and 20x3) will be shown as 100 percent.

9. COMMON-SIZE BALANCE SHEETS

Using the revisions to the 20x4 balance sheet given in Assignment 7, prepare common-size balance sheets for 20x4 and 20x3.

10. HORIZONTAL ANALYSIS OF INCOME STATEMENTS

Prepare a horizontal analysis of the following comparative income statement of Dynasty International. Round percentage changes to the nearest one-tenth percent (three decimal places):

Dynasty International
Comparative Income Statement
Years Ended December 31, 20x9 and 20x8

	20x9	20x8
Total revenue............................	$410,000	$373,000
Expenses:		
Cost of goods sold.................	$202,000	$188,000
Selling and general expenses..	98,000	93,000
Interest expense......................	7,000	4,000
Income tax expense................	42,000	37,000
Total expenses........................	349,000	322,000
Net income.............................	$ 61,000	$ 51,000

Why did net income increase by a higher percentage than total revenues during 20x9?

11.   CASH BUDGET

Create a worksheet of the following cash budget:

	MARCH	APRIL
Cash balance, beginning	$10,000	$29,500
Cash collections from customers	25,000	15,000
Sale of an asset	12,000	0
Total Available	$47,000	$44,500
Cash disbursements:		
Purchases	$12,000	$ 8,000
Operating expenses	5,500	2,225
Total Disbursements	$17,500	$10,225
Cash balance, ending	$29,500	$34,275

12.   CASH BUDGET

Refer to the previous assignment, but assume that the beginning cash balance on March 1 is now $15,000 and purchases are $10,000 (not $8,000) in April. Recompute the cash budget.

13.   BANK RECONCILIATION

D.J. Hunter's checkbook lists the following:

Date	Check No.	Item	Check	Deposit	Balance
9/1					$ 525
4	622	La Petite French Bakery	$ 19		506
9		Dividends Received		$ 116	622
13	623	General Tire Co.	43		579
14	624	Exxon Oil Co.	58		521
18	625	Cash	50		471
26	626	Fellowship Bible Church	25		446
28	627	Bent Tree Apartments	275		171
30		Paycheck		1,800	1,971

Hunter's September bank statement shows the following:

Balance			$525
Add: Deposits			116
Deduct checks:	No.	Amount	
	622	$19	
	623	43	
	624	68*	
	625	50	(180)

Other charges:		
Printed checks	$ 8	
Service charge	12	(20)
Balance		$441

*This is the correct amount for check number 624.
Prepare Hunter's bank reconciliation at September 30.

14. CASH BUDGET

Suppose Sprint Incorporated, the long-distance telephone company, is preparing its cash budget for 20x4. The company ended 20x3 with $126 million, and top management forsees the need for a cash balance of at least $125 million to pay all bills as they come due in 20x4.

Collections from customers are expected to total $11,813 million during 20x4, and payments for the cost of services and products should reach $6,166 million. Operating expense payments are budgeted at $2,744 million.

During 20x4, Sprint expects to invest $1,826 million in new equipment, $275 million in the company's cellular division, and to sell older assets for $116 million. Debt payments scheduled for 20x4 will total $597 million. The company forecasts net income of $890 million for 20x4 and plans to pay $338 million to its owners.

Prepare Sprint's cash budget for 20x4. Will the budgeted level of cash receipts leave Sprint with the desired ending cash balance of $125 million, or will the company need additional financing?

15.   BAD DEBT EXPENSE

Use the following information to calculate bad debt expense for 20x1:

Age of Accounts	A/R Balance	Percent Uncollectible
Under 30 days	$45,000	1%
31-60 days	25,000	3%
61-120 days	15,000	10%
Over 120 days	10,000	30%
Total	$95,000	

Prepare a worksheet demonstrating your computations.

16.   BAD DEBT EXPENSE

Now, assume that bad debt expense is 1% of credit sales. Using the following information, design a worksheet to calculate bad debt expense for 20x1:

Sales during 20x1:		
	Cash Sales	$100,000
	Credit Sales	200,000
	Total Sales	$300,000

17.   AGING SALES INVOICES

Design a worksheet which will enable the user to enter information from uncollected sales invoices. The information should include invoice number, date, amount, firm, and term. The worksheet should be able to calculate the number of days past due for each invoice (account receivable). It should also produce an aging schedule based on days past due. You need to include a line for the current date on the worksheet. You can use the command "=today( )" to make this always show the actual date, but we will enter the date so that it can be changed manually. In future assignments, we will experiment with different dates to see what happens with the aging analysis. For this assignment, use 11/15/03 as the date. Enter the date as "=date(03,11,15)."

A simple formula should be used to find the number of days outstanding for each receivable. To do this, simply subtract the sales invoice date from the current date shown on the worksheet. This will indicate the number of days that have elapsed since the invoice date; then subtract this number from the number of days in the term (e.g. 30 or 60, as in n/30 or n/60). The result is the number of days past due. Last, sort the invoices by days past due.

The input area should include the following uncollected invoices:

	A	B	C	D	E	F	G	H	I
9	Input Area:								
10	Date:	11/15/03							
11									
12	Invoice #	Date	Amount	Firm		Terms			
13	225	5/25/03	$950	blue	1	10 N		60	
14	301	6/17/03	235	red	2	10 N		60	
15	302	7/2/03	340	red	2	10 N		60	
16	303	7/3/03	560	blue	1	10 N		60	
17	307	8/18/03	270	pink		N		60	
18	309	9/15/03	880	pink		N		30	
19	312	9/22/03	1690	blue	1	10 N		60	
20	317	10/2/03	120	pink		N		30	
21	318	10/3/03	490	pink		N		30	
22	319	10/7/03	460	blue	1	10 N		60	

Use the following layout for the output area:

	A	B	C	D	E	F	G	H	I	J
25	Output Area:									
26										
27									Days	Days
28	Invoice #	Date	Amount	Firm		Terms			O/S	Past Due
29	225	5/25/03	$950	blue	1	10 N		60	174	114
30										

18.   AGING SALES INVOICES

Same as the prior assignment, but in the output area, add a row at the bottom showing average days for terms, days outstanding, and days past due.

19.   AGING SALES INVOICES

Using the worksheet created in Assignment 17, change the date to November 1, 2003. Print the revised aging schedule.

20.   ATTRIBUTE SAMPLING: DETERMINING SAMPLE SIZE

Assume that you are an auditor who is currently reviewing the internal controls structure of your client. Before vendor invoices are paid, the Treasurer is required to examine the voucher package for completeness and accuracy. The voucher package includes the following related documents: voucher, purchase order, purchase requisition, receiving report, and vendor invoice. At the time the check is prepared, the voucher package is stamped "paid." Your job is to determine if this internal control procedure is being followed. You will use attribute sampling to do so. The first step is to select a sample of voucher packages to examine.

Use the procedure described in the book website's example file: ATTRIB. Determine sample size if reliability is set at 95 percent, expected rate of occurrences (ERO) is 3 percent, and tolerable rate of occurrences (TRO) is 10 percent. Print results (output area of ATTRIB file).

21.   ATTRIBUTE SAMPLING: DETERMINING SAMPLE SIZE

Use the scenario described in the prior assignment but TRO is decreased from 10 percent to 6 percent. (The solution is shown at the end of this book.)

22.   ATTRIBUTE SAMPLING: EVALUATING RESULTS

Using the scenario in Assignment 20, assume that the correct sample size is 300, and TRO is 8 percent. If 18 errors (e.g. a missing document) are found, what is the auditor's conclusion regarding the effectiveness of the control? Use the procedure described in the example file: ATTRIB. Print results (output area of ATTRIB file).

23.   ATTRIBUTE SAMPLING: EVALUATING RESULTS

Same as previous assignment except that 25 errors are found. (The solution is shown at the end of this book.)

24.   ATTRIBUTE SAMPLING: EVALUATING RESULTS

Use the same scenario as described in Assignment 22 but TRO is decreased from 8 percent to 6 percent and only 9 errors are found.

25. VARIABLES SAMPLING: DETERMINING SAMPLE SIZE

Assume that you are an auditor who is examining the inventory account balance. The book value of inventory, as shown on the balance sheet, is $1,000,000. There are 1,000 inventory accounts. The auditor has set tolerable error (TE) at $100,000; the risk of incorrect rejection (IR) at 10 percent; the risk of incorrect acceptance (IA) at 5 percent; and estimated standard deviation at $300. Your job is to determine if inventory is fairly stated. You will use variables sampling to do so. The first step is to select a sample of inventory items. Use the procedure described in the book website's example file: VARIABLE (part one). Determine sample size. Print results (input/output area of part one). (The solution is shown at the end of this book.)

26. VARIABLES SAMPLING: DETERMINING SAMPLE SIZE

Same as previous assignment but IR is changed from 10 percent to 5 percent.

27. VARIABLES SAMPLING: DETERMINING SAMPLE SIZE

Use the scenario described in Assignment 25, but IR is changed from 10 percent to 5 percent and estimated standard deviation is changed from $300 to $200.

28. VARIABLES SAMPLING: EVALUATING RESULTS

Assume that you are an auditor. You are using variables sampling to determine if inventory is fairly stated on the financial statements. The client's book value of inventory is $1,000,000 and there are 1,000 inventory items. Assume that sample size has been correctly determined to be 81 items. The sample has been selected. The sample standard deviation is $9 and the sample mean is $980. The risk of incorrect rejection (IR) is set at 20 percent. Use the procedure described in the book website's example file: VARIABLE (part two). Determine whether you should accept or reject the client's book value of inventory. Print results (input/output area of part two).

29. VARIABLES SAMPLING: EVALUATING RESULTS

Same as previous assignment but IR is reduced from 20 percent to 10 percent and the sample mean is changed from $980 to $999. (The solution is shown at the end of this book.)

30.   VARIABLES SAMPLING: EVALUATING RESULTS

Use the same scenario described in Assignment 28, but IR is 5 percent and the sample mean is $1,003.

31.   PRODUCT MIX ANALYSIS

Four Seasons Fashions sells both designer and moderately priced women's wear. Profits have fluctuated recently, and top management is deciding which product line to emphasize. Accountants have provided the following data:

	Per Item	
	Designer	Moderately Priced
Average sale price	$200	$80
Average variable expenses	70	24
Average contribution margin	$130	$56
Average fixed expenses (allocated)	20	10
Average gross margin	$110	$46

The Four Seasons store in Boca Raton, Florida, has 10,000 square feet of floor space. If it emphasizes moderately priced goods, 500 items can be displayed in the store. In contrast, if it emphasizes designer wear, only 200 designer items can be displayed for sale. These numbers are also the average monthly sales in units.

Prepare product mix analysis that identifies which product to emphasize (i.e., the product with the highest total contribution margin).

Optional What-if Scenario:
What happens when the unit contribution margin for a moderately priced item is changed from $56 to $46?

32.   MAKE OR BUY ANALYSIS

Skiptronics Industrial Controls manufactures an electronic control that it uses in its final product. The electronic control has the following manufacturing costs per unit:

Direct materials	$ 5.00
Direct labor	1.00
Variable overhead	1.50
Fixed overhead	4.00
Manufacturing product cost	$11.50

An outside supplier can sell Skiptronics the electronic control for $8 per unit. If Skiptronics buys the control from the outside supplier, the manufacturing facilities that will be idled cannot be used for any other purpose. Should Skiptronics make or buy the electronic controls? Explain the difference between correct analysis and incorrect analysis of this decision.

Optional What-if Scenario:
What is the impact of changing the purchase price from $8 to $6?

33.   BEST USE OF FACILITIES ANALYSIS

Assume that Skiptronics can make the electronic control unit (which it uses in its final product) for an incremental cost of $7.50 or purchase the unit from an outside supplier for $8.00. Skiptronics needs 90,000 electronic controls. By purchasing them from the outside supplier, Skiptronics can use its idle facilities to manufacture another product that will contribute $75,000 to operating income. Identify the *incremental* costs that Skiptronics will incur to acquire 90,000 electronic controls under three alternative plans: (a) make the controls; (b) buy the controls and leave the facilities idle; or (c) buy the controls and use facilities to manufacture another product. Which plan makes the best use of Skiptronic's facilities? Prepare a worksheet to support your answer.

Optional What-if Scenario:
What is the impact of changing the incremental cost of buying from $8 to $8.50?

34.   SALES BY PRODUCT TYPE

Using the data below in the input area, prepare a new report sorted by current-month sales.

SALES SUMMARY REPORT BY PRODUCT TYPE FOR FEBRUARY

Product Type	Current Month Sales	Prior Month Sales	% Chg.	Year to Date Sales	Last Yr. YTD Sales	% Chg.
A	16	25	-36%	80	100	-20%
B	52	45	16%	260	234	11%
C	44	32	38%	220	154	43%
D	72	67	7%	360	333	8%
E	35	37	-5%	175	180	-3%

35.   COST-VOLUME-PROFIT ANALYSIS

Prepare a worksheet that illustrates cost-volume-profit (CVP) analysis, also referred to as break-even analysis. Use the following formulas:

CMU = SPU - VCU
Where: CMU is contribution margin per unit.
         SPU is sales price per unit.
         VCU is variable cost per unit.

BEP (units) = TFC / CMU
Where: TFC is total fixed cost.
         CMU is contribution margin per unit.

Assume that sales price per unit is $10; that variable cost per unit is $8; and that total fixed cost is $24,000. Calculate the contribution margin per unit, the break-even point in units of sales, and the break-even point in dollars of sales. (The solution is shown at the end of this book.)

36.   COST-VOLUME-PROFIT ANALYSIS

Same as previous assignment except that the sales price per unit is increased from $10 to $12.

37.   COST-VOLUME-PROFIT ANALYSIS: GRAPH

Assume that sales price per unit is $12, variable cost per unit is $8, and total fixed cost is $24,000. Prepare a line graph to illustrate break-even analysis. To prepare the graph, first set up a table with columns for units, total fixed cost (TFC), total variable cost (TVC), total cost (TC), sales revenue, and profit. In the units column, show values from zero to 8,000, in increments of 1000. Graph the data in columns for total fixed cost, total cost, and sales revenue. The formula for a line is typically expressed as y = a + bx. Applying this to our three lines, the formulas could be expressed as follows:

TFC = $24,000 + $0 * units
TC = $24,000 + $8 * units
Sales Revenue = $0 + $12 * units

Note: An example breakeven graph is available on the book website.

38.   COST-VOLUME-PROFIT ANALYSIS: GRAPH

Same as previous assignment, but change total fixed cost from $24,000 to $10,000.

39.   CONTRIBUTION MARGIN INCOME STATEMENT

Saville Row Shirtmakers' April income statement follows:

Saville Row Shirtmakers
Income Statement
April 20XX

Sales revenue		$640,000
Cost of goods sold		448,000
Gross margin		192,000
Operating expenses:		
Marketing expense	$72,000	
General and administrative expense	42,000	114,000
Operating income		$ 78,000

Saville Row's cost of goods sold is a variable expense. Marketing expense is 20% fixed and 80% variable. General and administrative expense is 60% fixed and 40% variable. Prepare Saville Row's contribution margin income statement for April. On the contribution margin income statement, include total sales revenue, total variable expenses, total contribution margin, total fixed expenses, and operating income. Calculate the expected increase in operating income to the nearest $1,000 if sales increase by $50,000.

Optional What-if Scenario:
What is the impact of changing the sales revenue from $640,000 to $740,000?

40.   DEPARTMENTAL INCOME STATEMENT

Portland Gear has two departments, Electronics and Industrial. The company's income statement for 20XX appears as follows:

Net sales.............................	$350,000
Cost of goods sold..............	116,000
Gross margin	234,000

Operating expenses:...........	
Salaries expense	$ 75,000
Depreciation expense	15,000
Advertising expense	6,000
Other expenses	10,000
Total operating expenses..	106,000
Operating income..............	$128,000

Sales are Electronics, $136,000 and Industrial, $214,000. Cost of goods sold is distributed $42,000 to Electronics and $74,000 to Industrial. Salaries are traced directly to departments: Electronics, $33,000; Industrial, $42,000. Electronics accounts for 80% of advertising. Depreciation is allocated on the basis of square footage: Electronics has 20,000 square feet; Industrial has 40,000 square feet. Other expenses are allocated based on the number of employees. An equal number of employees work in each of the two departments.

A   Prepare departmental income statements that show revenues, expenses, and operating income for each of the company's two departments.

B.   In a departmental performance report, which are the most important expenses for evaluating Portland Gear's department managers? Give your reason.

Optional What-if Scenario:
What happens when sales revenue in Electronics is increased to $144,000 along with an increase of sales revenue in Industrial to $256,000? (All other items are unchanged.)

41.   CASH DISBURSEMENTS

During February, PanAm Imports had the following transactions:

Feb.	3	Paid $392 on account to Marquis Corp. net of an $8 discount for an earlier purchase of inventory.
	6	Purchased inventory for cash, $1,267.
	11	Paid $375 for supplies.
	15	Purchased inventory on credit from Monroe Corporation, $774.
	16	Paid $4,062 on account to LaGrange Associates; there was no discount.
	21	Purchased furniture for cash, $960.
	26	Paid $3,910 on account to Graff Software for an earlier purchase of inventory. The discount was $90.
	27	Made a semiannual interest payment of $800 on a long-term note payable. The entire payment was for interest.

1. Prepare a cash disbursement journal similar to the one illustrated below. As shown, the check number (Ck. No.) and posting reference (Post. Ref.) columns are not included. Record the transactions in the journal.
2. Which transaction should not be recorded in the cash disbursements journal? In what journal does it belong?
3. Total the amount columns of the journal. Determine that the total debits equal the total credits.

Solution Started:

Cash Disbursements Journal						
			Debits		Credits	
Date		Account Debited	Other Accounts	Accounts Payable	Inventory	Cash
Feb.	3	Marquis Corp.		400	8	392

42. COST OF MERCHANDISE

Design a worksheet which will compute the cost of merchandise purchased. The worksheet should show the cost with and without the discount. The discount should be shown as the difference between these two amounts. Assume that you have purchased merchandise with a gross price of $5,000. This merchandise is subject to a trade discount of 30%. The trade discount is subtracted from the gross price to determine your actual purchase price. The credit terms offered to your company are 2/10, net 30. What is the amount due assuming that you do not take advantage of the discount period? What do you owe if you do take advantage of the discount?

43. COST OF MERCHANDISE

Same as previous assignment, but use $10,000 worth of merchandise rather than $5,000.

44. TRACKING INVENTORY QUANTITY

Design a worksheet which will enable you to enter inventory data. The information should include an item number, description, quantity on hand, and quantity desired. The worksheet should then calculate the amount by which the quantity on hand is above or below the desired quantity by use of a formula. Use the following information to complete the worksheet:

Item No	Description	Quantity on hand	Quantity desired
100	HAMMER	8	30
200	SCREWDRIVER	26	20
300	SAW	57	45
400	WRENCH	34	20
500	PLIERS	5	15

45.   PRODUCT COST SCHEDULE

Prepare a cost schedule for Austin Company for Product X and Product Y using the following layout:

(Input Area)	Product X	Product Y
Total Units		
DM Cost/Unit		
DL Cost/Unit		
OH allocation rate		
Total OH (X & Y)		

(Output Area)

Company Name
Product Cost Schedule
Date

	Product X	Product Y
Direct Materials		
Direct Labor		
Manufacturing Overhead		
Total Cost		

The costs of the direct material for the two products are $2.00 per unit for X and $3.00 per unit for Y. The direct labor costs are $.25 per unit produced for either product. The total manufacturing overhead for the year is $300,000. This should be allocated to the different products based on the ratio of each product's production to total production. Austin Company produced 100,000 units of product X and 50,000 units of product Y.

46.   PERPETUAL INVENTORY RECORD

Piazza Music World carries a large inventory of guitars, keyboards, and other musical instruments. Because each item is expensive, Piazza uses a perpetual inventory system.

Company records indicate the following for a particular line of Casio keyboards:

Date	Item	Quantity	Unit Cost
May 1	Balance	5	$90
6	Sale	3	
8	Purchase	11	95
17	Sale	4	
30	Sale	1	

Determine the amounts that Piazza should report for ending inventory and cost of goods sold by the FIFO method. Prepare the perpetual inventory record for Casio keyboards, using the model that follows.

Perpetual Inventory Record – FIFO Cost

Hunting Galleries										
Item: Early American Chairs										
	Received			Sold			Balance			
Date	Qty.	Unit Cost	Total	Qty.	Unit Cost	Total	Qty.	Unit Cost	Total	
Nov.										
1							10	$300	$3,000	
5				6	$300	$ 1,800	4	300	1,200	
7	25	$310	$7,750				4	300	1,200	
							25	310	7,750	
12				4	300	1,200				
				9	310	2,790	16	310	4,960	
26	25	320	8,000				16	310	4,960	
							25	320	8,000	
30				16	310	4,960				
				5	320	1,600	20	320	6,400	
Totals:	50		$15,750	40		$12,350	20		$6,400	

47. INCOME STATEMENT, BALANCE SHEET, AND STATEMENT OF CASH FLOWS

Campbell Soup Company uses a perpetual inventory system and the LIFO method to determine the cost of its inventory. During a recent year, Campbell Soup reported the following items in its financial statements, year ended July 31, 20x5 (listed in alphabetical order, and with amounts given in millions of dollars).

Collections from customers	$7,255	Payments for inventory	$4,150
Cost of goods sold	4,264	Revenues, total	7,288

Other expenses	2,326	Total assets	6,315
Owners' equity	2,468	Total liabilities	3,847

1. Prepare as much of Campbell Soup Company's statement of cash flows for the year ended July 31, 20x5, as you can. Include a complete heading.
2. Prepare Campbell Soup Company's income statement for the year ended July 31, 20x5, complete with a heading.
3. Prepare Campbell Soup Company's balance sheet at July 31, 20x5, complete with a heading.

48. COST ALLOCATION RATES

Chromium Ltd. uses activity-based costing for its manufacturing process. Company managers have identified four manufacturing activities: materials handling, machine setup, insertion of parts, and finishing. The budgeted activity costs for 20X1 and their allocation bases are as follows:

Activity	Total Budgeted Cost	Allocation Base
Materials handling	$12,000	Number of parts
Machine setup	2,400	Number of setups
Insertion of parts	24,000	Number of parts
Finishing	60,000	Finishing direct labor-hours
Total	$98,400	

Chromium expects to produce 2,000 chrome wheels during the year. The wheels are expected to use 12,000 parts, require 6 setups, and consume 1,000 hours of finishing time.

A. Compute the cost allocation rate for each activity.
B. Compute the indirect manufacturing cost of each wheel.

Optional What-if Scenario:
What is the impact of changing the materials handling cost from $12,000 to $6,000?

49. BUDGETED COSTS: ABC COST PER UNIT

Several years after re-engineering its production process, Chromex hired a new controller, Rebecca Steinberg. She developed an ABC system very similar to the one used by Chromex's chief rival, Chromium, Ltd., described above. Part of the reason Steinberg developed the ABC system was that Chromex's profits had been declining, even though the company had shifted its product mix toward the product that had appeared most profitable under the old system. Before adopting the new ABC system, Chromex had used a direct labor hour single-allocation-base system that was developed 20 years ago.

For 20X1, Chromex's budgeted ABC allocation rates are:

Activity	Allocation Base	Cost Allocation Rate
Materials handling	Number of parts	$ 1.25 per part
Machine setup	Number of setups	300.00 per setup
Insertion of parts	Number of parts	3.00 per part
Finishing	Finishing direct labor-hours	70.00 per hour

The number of parts is now a feasible allocation base because Chromex recently purchased bar coding technology. Chromex produces two wheel models: standard and deluxe. Budgeted data for 20X1 are as follows:

	Standard	Deluxe
Parts per Unit	5.0	7.0
Setups Per 1,000 units	3.0	3.0
Finishing direct labor hours per unit	0.2	1.0
Total direct labor hours per unit	2.0	3.0

The company's managers expect to produce 1,000 units of each model during the year.

A. Compute the total budgeted cost for 20X1.
B. Compute the ABC cost per unit of each model.
C. Using Chromex's old direct labor hour single allocation-base system, compute the (single) allocation rate based on direct labor hours. Use this rate to determine the cost per wheel for each model under the old single-allocation-base method.

Optional What-if Scenario:
What is the impact of changing the materials handling allocation rate from $1.25 to $2.00?

Note: The solution to the first part of this assignment is shown at the end of the book. The solution to the "what-if" scenario is not shown.

50. MANUFACTURING COST BASED ON ABC UNIT COST

For 20X2, Chromex's managers have determined the following conversion costs per wheel: ABC (indirect) cost per standard wheel is $36.15 and per deluxe wheel is $100.65; alternatively, single-rate (indirect) cost per standard wheel is $54.72 and per deluxe wheel is $82.08. In addition to the unit conversion costs, the following data are budgeted for the company's standard and deluxe models for 20X2:

	Standard	Deluxe
Sale price	$110.00	$155.00
Direct materials	15.00	25.00

Because of limited machine hour capacity, Chromex can produce either 2,000 standard wheels or 2,000 deluxe wheels.

A. If the managers rely on the ABC unit cost data, which model will they produce? Show support for your answer. (All non-manufacturing costs are the same for both models.)

B. If the managers rely on the single-allocation-base cost data, which model will they produce? Show support for your answer.

C. Which course of action will yield more income for Chromex? Show support for your answer.

Optional What-if Scenario:
What is the impact of changing the sales price of the standard model from $110 to $75?

51.   UNITS-OF-PRODUCTION DEPRECIATION

Create a worksheet which will calculate deprecation on a machine based on the units-of-production method of depreciation. Assume that you bought a machine on January 1 of Year 1 for $150,000. It has a $2,000 salvage value and a useful life of 100,000 units. Calculate the depreciation expense, accumulated depreciation, and net machine (cost less accumulated depreciation) that would be shown on the balance sheet for the first three years of use based on the following information:

	UNITS PRODUCED
1st year	15,000
2nd year	20,000
3rd year	18,000

52.   JOINT COST ALLOCATION

You are performing an audit on a small company and must ensure that the total joint costs are allocated correctly among the three products of the company. Use the following information to compute the cost allocated to each product. NOTE: Total costs to be allocated are $450,000.

Product	Sales Value at Split-Off
A	$500,000
B	300,000
C	200,000

Prepare a worksheet demonstrating your computations.

53.   JOINT COST ALLOCATION

Referring to the prior assignment, calculate the joint costs to be allocated to the three products assuming that total costs are $600,000 and the sales values at split-off are as follows:

Product	Sales Value at Split-off
A	$800,000
B	500,000
C	700,000

54.   ALLOCATION OF COSTS IN LUMP-SUM PURCHASE

Advantage Leasing Company bought three used machines in a $40,000 lump-sum purchase. An independent appraiser valued the machines as follows:

Machine No.	Appraised Value
1	14,000
2	18,000
3	16,000

Advantage paid half in cash and signed a note payable for the remainder. Record the purchase in the journal, identifying each machine's individual cost in a separate Machine account. Round decimals to three places.

55.   STATEMENT OF OWNERS' EQUITY

Use the data shown below to prepare the statement of owner's equity of On-Point Delivery

Service for the year ended December 31, 20x3. Follow the format shown in Exhibit B of Assignment 3.

Salary expense	$32,000	Insurance expense	$ 4,000
Accounts payable	7,000	Service revenue	91,000
Owner, capital		Accounts receivable	17,000
Dec. 31, 20x2	13,000	Supplies expense	1,000
Supplies	2,000	Cash	5,000
Withdrawals by owner	36,000	Fuel expense	6,000
Rent expense	8,000		

56. PREPARATION OF ADJUSTED TRIAL BALANCE

The adjusted trial balance of Total Express Service is incomplete. Enter the adjustment amounts directly in the adjustment columns. Service Revenue is the only account affected by more than one adjustment.

Total Express Service Preparation of Adjusted Trial Balance May 31, 20X2						
	Trial Balance		Adjustments		Adjusted Trial Balance	
Account Title	Debit	Credit	Debit	Credit	Debit	Credit
Cash	3,000				3,000	
Accounts receivable	6,500				7,100	
Supplies	1,040				800	
Office furniture	32,300				32,300	
Accumulated depreciation		14,040				14,400
Salary payable						900
Unearned revenue		900				690
Capital		26,360				26,360
Owner's withdrawals	6,000				6,000	
Service revenue		11,630				12,440
Salary expense	2,690				3,590	
Rent expense	1,400				1,400	
Depreciation expense					360	
Supplies expense					240	
	52,930	52,930			54,790	54,790

57.   FINANCIAL STATEMENTS AND RELATED QUESTIONS

The adjusted trial balance of Tradewind Travel Designers at December 31, 20x6 follows:

Tradewind Travel Designers
Adjusted Trial Balance
December 31, 20x6

Cash	$ 1,320	
Accounts receivable	8,920	
Supplies	2,300	
Prepaid rent	1,600	
Office equipment	20,180	
Accumulated depreciation-office equipment		$ 4,350
Office furniture	37,710	
Accumulated depreciation-office furniture		4,870
Accounts payable		3,640
Property tax payable		1,100
Interest payable		830
Unearned service revenue		620
Note payable		13,500
Gary Gillen, capital		26,090
Gary Gillen, withdrawals	29,000	
Service revenue		124,910
Depreciation expense-office equipment	6,680	
Depreciation expense-office furniture	2,370	
Salary expense	39,900	
Rent expense	17,400	
Interest expense	3,100	
Utilities expense	2,670	
Insurance expense	3,810	
Supplies expense	2,950	
Total	$179,910	$179,910

Prepare Tradewind's 20x6 income statement and statement of owner's equity and year-end balance sheet. List expenses in decreasing order on the income statement and show total liabilities on the balance sheet.

1.   Which financial statement reports Tradewind Travel's results of operations? Were operations successful during 20x6? Cite specifics from the financial statements to support your evaluation.

2.   Which statement reports the company's financial position? Does Tradewind's financial position look strong or weak? Give the reason for your evaluation.

58.   POST-CLOSING TRIAL BALANCE

After closing its accounts at December 31, 20x6, Sprint Corporation had the following account balances, with amounts given in millions:

Property and equipment	$10,464	Long-term liabilities	$5,119
Cash	1,150	Other assets	2,136
Service revenue	-0-	Accounts receivable	2,464
Owners' equity	8,520	Total expenses	-0-
Other current assets	739	Accounts payable	1,027
Short-term notes payable	200	Other current liabilities .	2,087

Prepare Sprint's post-closing trial balance at December 31, 20x6. List accounts in proper order, like the trial balance shown below.

Gary Lyon, CPA
Postclosing Trial Balance
April 30, 20x1

Cash	$24,800	
Accounts receivable	2,500	
Supplies	400	
Prepaid rent	2,000	
Furniture	16,500	
Accumulated depreciation		$ 275
Accounts payable		13,100
Salary payable		950
Unearned service revenue		300
Gary Lyon, capital		31,575
Total	$46,200	$46,200

59. TRIAL BALANCE AND WORKSHEET

The trial balance of Goldsmith Testing Service follows:

Goldsmith Testing Service
Trial Balance
September 30, 20x6

Cash	$ 3,560	
Accounts receivable	3,440	
Prepaid rent	1,200	
Supplies	3,390	
Equipment	32,600	
Accumulated depreciation		$ 2,840
Accounts payable		3,600
Salary payable		
L. Goldsmith, capital		36,030
L. Goldsmith, withdrawals	3,000	
Service revenue		7,300
Depreciation expense		
Salary expense	1,800	
Rent expense		
Utilities expense	780	
Supplies expense		
Total	$49,770	$49,770

Additional Information at September 30, 20x6:
  (a) Accrued service revenue, $210.
  (b) Depreciation, $40.
  (c) Accrued salary expense, $500.
  (d) Prepaid rent expired, $600.
  (e) Supplies used, $1,650.

Complete Goldsmith's worksheet (on the following page) for September 20x6.

Account Title	Trial Balance		Adjust-ments		Adjusted Trial Bal.		Income Statement		Balance Sheet	
Goldsmith Testing Service										
Work Sheet										
Month Ended September 30, 20X6										
Cash	Dr.	Cr.	Dr.	Cr.	Dr.	Cr.	Dr.	Cr.	Dr.	Cr.
Accounts receivable										
Prepaid rent										
Supplies										
Equipment										
Accumulated depreciation										
Accounts payable										
Salary payable										
L. Goldsmith, capital										
L. Goldsmith, withdrawals										
Service revenue										
Depreciation expense										
Salary expense										
Rent expense										
Utilities expense										
Supplies expense										
Totals										
Net income										
Totals (IS, BS)										

60. BOND AMORTIZATION SCHEDULE

Atlas Airlines, Inc., issued $600,000 of 8-3/8% (0.08375), five-year bonds payable when the market interest rate was 9-1/2% (0.095). Atlas pays interest annually at year end. The issue price of the bonds was $574,082.

Create a spreadsheet model to amortize the discount on these bonds. Use the effective-interest method of amortization. Round to the nearest dollar, and format your answer as follows:

	A	B	C	D	E	F
11	Output Area:					
12						Bond
13		Interest	Interest	Discount	Discount	Carrying
14	Date	Payment	Expense	Amortization	Balance	Amount
15	1-1-x1				$	$574,082
16	12-31-x1	$	$	$		$
17	12-31-x2					
18	12-31-x3					
19	12-31-x4					
20	12-31-x5					

Use the following formulas:

Interest payment (B16):	=600000*.08375
Interest expense (C16):	=F15*.095
Discount amortization (D16):	=C16-B16
Discount balance (E15):	=600000-F15
Bond carrying amount (F16):	=F15+D16

Background for Assignments 61 to 71: Foreign Currency Translation

When a multinational corporation based in the U.S. owns more than 50 percent of the voting stock of a foreign company, a parent-subsidiary relationship exists. The parent company is usually required to prepare consolidated financial statements. Before this can be done, the financial statements of the foreign subsidiary must be recast using U.S. generally accepted accounting principles (GAAP). Next, the foreign accounts must be remeasured (translated) from the foreign currency into U.S. dollars. To make the translation, the first step is to identify three currencies:

(a)   Currency of books and records (CBR) -- the CBR is the currency in which the foreign financial statements is denominated;

(b)   Functional currency (FC) -- the FC is the one in which the subsidiary generally buys, sells, borrows, repays, etc.; and

(c)   Reporting currency (RC) -- the RC is the one in which the consolidated financial statements is denominated.

There are basically three approaches to currency translation: (1) temporal rate method, (2) current rate method, and (3) use of both methods. The following three rules are used to determine the method of translation:

Rule 1:   If the FC is hyper-inflationary (i.e., 100% cumulative inflation within three years), then ignore the FC and remeasure the CBR into the RC using the temporal rate method.

Rule 2:   If the CBR is different from the FC, then remeasure the CBR into the FC using the temporal rate method.

Rule 3:   Translate from the FC into the RC using the current rate method.

You must apply the rules in sequence, stopping when the subsidiary's financial statements have been converted into the parent's reporting currency (RC). For example, when the functional currency (FC) is hyper-inflationary, then Rule 1 applies; that is, the financial statements which are denominated in the CBR are translated into the RC using the temporal rate method, and Rules 2 and 3 aren't used. A second example is as follows: If the CBR is British pounds, the FC is Dutch guilders (not hyper-inflationary), and the RC is U.S. dollars, then you skip Rule 1 and apply Rule 2, translating the CBR (pounds) into the FC (guilders) using the temporal rate method. Since the FC (guilders) is not the RC (dollars), you would then apply Rule 3 to translate the FC (guilders) into the RC (dollars) using the current rate method. A third example is as follows: When the CBR is the same as the FC, then you go directly to Rule 3.

Using the current rate method, all assets and liabilities are translated using the current rate (i.e., exchange rate on the balance sheet date). Owners' equity and dividends are translated at historical rates (exchange rate at the time the asset was acquired, liability incurred, or element of paid-in capital was issued or reacquired). Income statement items can be translated using the average exchange rate (the average of the exchange rate at the beginning of the accounting period and the current rate).

Under the temporal rate method, the objective is to measure each subsidiary transaction as though the transaction had been made by the parent. Monetary items (e.g. cash, receivables, inventories carried at market, payables, and long-term debt) are re-measured using the current exchange rate. Other items (e.g. prepaid expenses, inventories carried at cost, fixed assets, and stock) are re-measured using historical exchange rates.

Since different exchange rates are applied to different accounts, the resulting dollar-denominated trial balance will not likely balance. The debit or credit required to bring the dollar-denominated accounts into balance is the "cumulative translation adjustment." The change in the cumulative translation adjustment during the current accounting period is the translation gain or loss. Under the current rate method, the translation gain or loss is accumulated on a separate line in the owner's equity section of the balance sheet and has no impact on the income statement. Under the temporal rate method, the translation gain or loss is shown on the income statement.

61. FOREIGN CURRENCY TRANSLATION USING THE CURRENT RATE METHOD

First, read the background information for this problem starting on page 87 . Translate the following account balances from Dutch guilders to U.S. dollars using the current rate method.

Adjusted Trial Balance
In Dutch Guilders (DG)
December 31, Year 4

	Debit	Credit
Cash	20,000	
Accounts Receivable	35,000	
Inventory	105,000	
Equipment	60,000	
Accum. Dep.		20,000
Accounts Payable		35,000
Bonds Payable		50,000
Revenues		120,000
General Expenses	108,000	
Depreciation Expense	8,000	
Dividends	4,000	
Common Stock		62,000
Paid-in Capital in Excess of Par		44,000
Retained Earnings		9,000
Total	340,000	340,000

Exchange Rates:

	1 DG = $____
Current Exchange Rate	0.520
Average Exchange Rate	0.490
At July 31, Year 4	0.505
At June 30, Year 1	0.470

Other: All common stock was issued on June 30, Year 1 (i.e., 6/30/Y1).
Dividends were declared and paid on July 31, Year 4.
Translated Retained Earnings at 12/31/Y4 was: $5,500.

Note: The solution to this problem is at the end of the book.

62. FOREIGN CURRENCY TRANSLATION USING THE CURRENT RATE METHOD

Same as previous assignment, except the exchange rates are as follows:

Current Exchange Rate	1.200
Average Exchange Rate	1.250
At July 31, Year 4	1.300
At June 30, Year 1	1.000

63. FOREIGN CURRENCY TRANSLATION USING THE CURRENT RATE METHOD

Use the following information to translate from British pounds to U.S. dollars using the current rate method. Background information starts on page 87.

Adjusted Trial Balance
In British Pounds
December 31, Year 8

	Debit	Credit
Cash	72,000	
Accounts Receivable	60,000	
Inventory	136,000	
Fixed Assets	130,000	
Accum. Dep.		76,000
Accounts Payable		50,000
Bonds Payable		90,000
Revenues		172,000
General Expenses	158,000	
Depreciation Expense	10,000	
Dividends	4,000	
Common Stock		58,000
Paid-in Capital in Excess of Par		98,000
Retained Earnings		26,000
Total	570,000	570,000

Exchange Rates:

	1 BP = $____
Current Exchange Rate	2.100
Average Exchange Rate	2.000
At July 31, Year 8	2.050
At June 30, Year 1	1.500

Other: All common stock was issued on June 30, Year 1 (i.e., 6/30/Y1).
Dividends were declared and paid on July 31, Year 8.
Translated Retained Earnings at 12/31/Y8 was $22,600.

64. FOREIGN CURRENCY TRANSLATION USING THE CURRENT RATE METHOD

Same as previous assignment, except use the following exchange rates:

Current Exchange Rate	3.100
Average Exchange Rate	2.900
At July 31, Year 8	2.950
At June 30, Year 1	4.000

65. FOREIGN CURRENCY TRANSLATION USING THE TEMPORAL RATE METHOD

Use the temporal rate method to remeasure from the currency of books and records (i.e., British pounds) to the functional currency (i.e., U.S. dollars). Background information starts on page 87.

Adjusted Trial Balance
In British Pounds
December 31, Year 4

	Debit	Credit
Cash	52,000	
Accounts Receivable	60,000	
Inventory		
(10-31-Y3)	40,000	
(7-31-Y4)	160,000	

Adjusted Trial Balance - Continued

Fixed Assets		
(6-30-Y1)	13,000	
(12-31-Y1)	65,000	
(7-31-Y2)	52,000	
Accum. Dep.		
(6-30-Y1)		8,000
(12-31-Y1)		40,000
(7-31-Y2)		32,000
Accounts Payable		43,000
Bonds Payable		160,000
Revenues		214,000
General Expenses	189,000	
Depreciation Expense		
(6-30-Y1)	1,500	
(12-31-Y1)	7,500	
(7-31-Y2)	6,000	
Dividends (7-31-Y4)	10,000	
Common Stock		
(6-30-Y1)		48,000
(1-31-Y2)		32,000
Paid-in Capital in Excess of Par		
(6-30-Y1)		30,000
(1-31-Y2)		20,000
Retained Earnings		29,000
Total	656,000	656,000

Exchange Rates	1 BP = $___	
Current Exchange Rate		0.600
Average Exchange Rate		0.610
At July 31, Year 4		0.606
At October 31, Year 3		0.591
At July 31, Year 2		0.585
At January 31, Year 2		0.586
At December 31, Year 1		0.590
At June 30, Year 1		0.580

Other:

Regarding common stock, 60% was issued 6/30/Y1; 40% on 1/31/Y2.
Regarding inventory, 20% was acquired 10/31/Y3; 80% on 7/31/Y4.

Dividends were declared and paid on 7/31/Y4.
Regarding fixed assets, 10% were acquired 6/30/Y1; 50% on 12/31/Y1; and 40% on 7/31/Y2.
Revenues and expenses were accrued evenly throughout the year.
Translated retained earnings at 12/31/Y4 was $16,400

66. FOREIGN CURRENCY TRANSLATION USING THE TEMPORAL RATE METHOD

Same as previous assignment, except use the following exchange rates:

	1 BP = $____
Current Exchange Rate	2.000
Average Exchange Rate	2.400
At July 31, Year 4	2.300
At October 31, Year 3	2.150
At July 31, Year 2	2.200
At January 31, Year 2	2.180
At December 31, Year 1	2.250
At June 30, Year 1	2.100

Background for Assignments 67 to 71: Comparative Advantage

Productivity provides an economic basis for trade. During the early 1800s, David Ricardo and other economists provided an explanation for trade based on different levels of productivity among nations in different industries. This can be illustrated as follows. First, assume that there is only one factor of production, labor. Next, assume that a worker in the country of Bigred can produce either 8 bales of cotton or 4 crates of apples, and that a worker in the country of Bigblue can produce either 1 bale of cotton or 1 crate of apples. Table A shows production in Bigred and Bigblue.

Table A Cotton and Apples as Produced by Bigred and Bigblue		
	Bigred Worker	Bigblue Worker
Cotton	8 bales	1 bale
Apples	4 crates	1 crate

Opportunity costs of production are shown in Table B.

Table B
Opportunity Costs of Production in Bigred and Bigblue

Bigred: 8 bales of cotton cost 4 crates of apples, so
                   1 bale of cotton costs 1/2 crate of apples.
                   4 crates of apples cost 8 bales of cotton, so
                   1 crate of apples costs 2 bales of cotton.

Bigblue: 1 bale of cotton costs 1 crate of apples.
                   1 crate of apples costs 1 bale of cotton.

Table A shows that a worker in Bigred is more productive in both cotton and apples than a worker in Bigblue. The Bigred worker has an "absolute advantage" in productivity in both industries. When industries are compared, the Bigred worker is found to be relatively more productive in the cotton industry (8 to 1) than in the apple industry (4 to 1) in relation to the Bigblue worker. Thus, the Bigred worker has a "comparative advantage" in the cotton industry. Thus, Bigred's absolute advantage in cotton is proportionately greater than its absolute advantage in apples.

A lower skilled and lower productive nation will have a comparative advantage in something because there will be some industry in which it is least disadvantaged. If Bigred is better at producing apples than Bigblue, why won't Bigred produce its own apples? The answer is that Bigred determines it more advantageous to produce what it does best, cotton, and trading this cotton for apples. Table C, which is derived from Table B, shows what prices would have to be in effect for trade to be beneficial.

Table C
Prices at Which Trade Would Occur

Bigred: If 1 bale of cotton sells for more than 1/2 crate of apples, Bigred gains by selling cotton.

               If 1 crate of apples sells for less than 2 bales of cotton, Bigred gains by buying apples.

Bigblue: If 1 bale of cotton sells for less than 1 crate of apples, Bigblue gains by buying cotton.

               If 1 crate of apples sells for more than 1 bale of cotton, Bigblue gains by selling apples.

Thus: If the price of apples on the world markets is between 1 bale of cotton and 2 bales of cotton, and if the price of apples is between 1/2 crate of apples and 1 crate of apples, trade is mutually advantageous.

Table D shows the change in world output if firms in each nation reallocate workers to the industry in which the nation has a comparative advantage. The Bigred cotton industry hires a worker away from the apple industry, and the Bigblue apple industry hires five workers away from the cotton industry. Consequently, the world output of cotton increases by 3 bales, and the world output of apples increases by 1 crate.

Table D
Increase in World Production Based on Transfers of
One Worker in Bigred and Five Workers in Bigblue

	One Bigred Worker	Five Bigblue Workers	World Output
Cotton (bales)	+1	-5	+3
Apples (crates)	-1	+5	+1

Assume that the Bigred firm exports 4 bales of cotton to Bigblue, and that the price of a bale of cotton is 0.7 crates of apples. The trade yields Bigred 2.8 crates of apples. Before international trade, the Bigred firm could have obtained only 2 crates of apples for its 4 bales of cotton. Before international trade, the Bigblue could have obtained only 2.8 bales of cotton for its 2.8 crates of apples, but now gets 4 bales of cotton for its 2.8 crates. The price determines which country receives the greatest benefit. For example, if 1 bale of cotton equals to 0.8 crates of apples, Bigred would have benefitted more from the trade than where the price was 0.7 crates. However, as long at the price falls within the range shown in Table C, both countries gain from specialization and trade. If the costs of production of cotton and apples remained constant, eventually all cotton would be produced in Bigred and all apples in Bigblue. However, increasing costs will probably occur at some point; the cost of producing cotton in Bigred will increase, and the cost of producing apples in Bigblue will increase. At this point, trade is curtailed. Consequently, it is rarely the case that one country produces all of one product.

Effects of an Import Quota

Given the above presentation of comparative advantage, you can understand why the great majority of economists strongly support free trade and oppose the use of tariffs and quotas that impede the free exchange of goods and services. However, there are political motivations that advocate protection of domestic industry. The political motivations for advocating protectionism generally are not supported by sound economic analysis.

67.   ECONOMIC IMPACT OF AN IMPORT QUOTA

First, read the background information for this problem starting on page 93.
Use the following equation to prepare a domestic demand curve:

   $P(QD) = 100 - 10 * Q$

Use the following equations to prepare a domestic supply and a world supply curve:

   $P(QS\text{-}d) = 0 + 10 * Q$
   $P(QS\text{-}w) = 20 + 0*Q$

The demand curve represents the home country's demand for a homogeneous good (e.g. corn, iron, rubber, etc.). The domestic supply curve is a typical upward-sloping curve. The world market price is $20; thus, persons may import as much as they want at a constant price of $20. In other words, the world supply curve is perfectly elastic at a price of $20. Assume that an import quota of 4 units is established.

Prepare the following:

A.   Table of Q (from 0 to 10, in increments of 1), P(QD), P(QS-domestic), and P(QS-world).

B.   Graph the domestic demand curve (P(QD), domestic supply curve (P(QS-d), world supply curve (P(QS-w), and a vertical line at the quantity of 4 to illustrate the effect of the quota.

C.   What is equilibrium price and quantity before and after the quota?

D.   Who are the winners and losers from the quota?

Note: An example of the economic impact of an import quota is shown on the book website.

68.   ECONOMIC IMPACT OF AN IMPORT QUOTA

Same as previous assignment, except for the following changes:

1.   The demand equation is as follows: $P(QD) = 120 - 10*Q$
2.   The world market price is $30.
3.   The domestic supply and world supply equations are as follows:
         $P(QS\text{-}d) = 20 + 10*Q$
         $P(QS\text{-}w) = 30 + 0*Q$
4.   The quota is set at 3 units.

69.   ECONOMIC IMPACT OF A TARIFF

Read the background information for this assignment starting on page 93.
Use the following information and analyze the impact of a tariff. Use the following equation to prepare a domestic demand curve:

$$P(QD) = 120 - 1*Q$$

Use the following equations to prepare a supply curve before and after the tariff is implemented. The tariff is set at $20.

$$P(QS) = 20 + 1*Q$$
$$P(QS)+T = (20 + 1*Q) + T$$

Prepare the following:
A.   Table of Q (from 0 to 100, in increments of 10), P(QD), P(QS), and P(QS)+T.
B.   Graph of the demand curve, P(QD); supply curve before tariff, P(QS); and supply curve after tariff, P(QS)+T.
C.   What is equilibrium price and quantity before and after the tariff?
D.   What is the protective effect and revenue effect of the tariff?

Note: An example of the economic impact of an import quota is shown on the book website.

70.   ECONOMIC IMPACT OF A TARIFF

Same as previous assignment, except the tariff is set at $40 rather than $20.

71.   ECONOMIC IMPACT OF A TARIFF

Same as Assignment 69, except the tariff is set at $60 rather than $20.

72.   DOUBLE-ENTRY ACCOUNTING

Design a worksheet that enables the user to record transactions in general ledger accounts. Additionally, the worksheet should be designed so that the ending balances in the general ledger accounts are used to automatically prepare a trial balance and an income statement, which will be prepared in the next assignment. Use the same approach as shown in the example file, GLEDGER, which is available on the book's website. Starting with a zero balance in all general ledger accounts, enter the following transactions. Print the general ledger.

Straight line method

$$D = \frac{C - S_n}{n}$$

C = cost/present worth
S_n = expected salvage value in yr n
n = #compdg pds

Jan. 1:	Mary Smith opens a consulting firm with an $8,000 deposit into the firm's checking account.
Jan. 1:	Prepaid three months of rent for $1,500.
Jan. 2:	Borrowed $4,000 with a note payable to purchase a computer with a two-year useful life and a salvage value of $400.
Jan. 3:	Purchased office supplies on credit for $800.
Jan. 10:	Provided consulting services on account for $3,200.
Jan. 12:	Provided consulting services on account for $1,200.
Jan. 15:	Received partial payment of $1,600 for services rendered on account on January 10.
Jan. 20:	Provided consulting services on account for $2,000.
Jan. 25:	Paid telephone bill of $375.
Jan. 26:	Paid electric bill of $225.
Jan. 31:	Make adjusting entry to record expiration of one month of prepaid rent.
Jan. 31:	Make adjusting entry to record use of office supplies. One-half of supplies have been used.
Jan. 31:	Record depreciation on office equipment for one month. Use straight-line depreciation.
Jan. 31:	The owner, Mary Smith, withdraws $4,000 for personal use.

$$\frac{(4000 - 400)}{2} = 12$$

73. DOUBLE-ENTRY ACCOUNTING

Using information from the prior assignment, prepare the trial balance and income statement.

74. T-ACCOUNTS AND TRIAL BALANCE

Refer to the following transactions of Wellness Health Club.

Wellness Health Club Transactions

Wellness Health Club engaged in the following transactions during March 20x3, its first month of operations:

Mar. 1	Lou Stryker invested $45,000 of cash to start the business.
2	Purchased office supplies of $200 on account.
4	Paid $40,000 cash for a building to use as a future office.
6	Performed service for customers and received cash, $2,000.
9	Paid $100 on accounts payable.
17	Performed service for customers on account, $1,600.
23	Received $1,200 cash from a customer on account.

31   Paid the following expenses: salary, $1,200; rent, $500.

Record the preceding transactions in the journal of Wellness Health Club. Key transactions by date and include an explanation for each entry. Use the following accounts: Cash; Accounts Receivable; Office Supplies; Building; Accounts Payable; Lou Stryker, Capital; Service Revenue; Salary Expense; Rent Expense. (Hint: For help, refer to the example file, GLEDGER, on the website.)

1.   After journalizing the above transactions, post the entries to the ledger, using T-account format. Key transactions by date. Date the ending balance of each account Mar. 31.

2.   Prepare the trial balance of Wellness Health Club at March 31, 20x3.

Audit Case Problem

You are the new staff accountant for the audit firm of Smith, Kerr & Warren (SKW). Your first job is to assist on the year-end audit of Toy Co, Inc. This is February of 20x4 and you are working to finish the audit by the end of the month to present the financials for the year ended December 31, 20x3.

Toy Co, Inc. has been a client of SKW for about 10 years. They are a small toy company located in Smithville, USA. They hand craft wooden toy models of cars, tractors, trains, etc. The toys are elaborately detailed and require a great deal of craftsmanship including carving, building, and painting. The company takes specialized orders and makes each toy to those specifications. The toys are sold through special order only and are not mass produced. The sale price of each toy is between $45-$700 depending on the detail and work involved in production.

The company operates like other companies. Toy Co maintains standard insurance policies and has a few operating leases. The company carries some debt to finance slower times (the company is usually much busier during the Christmas holidays). The company has a building, office equipment, and some factory equipment to saw the boards needed for the projects. The firm cuts and ships its own wood for making the toys. The firm operates a small sawmill. Toy Co also maintains a warehouse to store its high quality lumber.

Your tasks for the audit are outlined in the work program for 20x3. The workprogram and all of the necessary worksheets are included in a file named AuditScheds.xls. In addition to the workprogram, there is a worksheet in the file called PBC which will contain all of the information that you will need from the client. A more senior member of the engagement team has already tied all of the numbers and information to source documents so that all you need to do is prepare the worksheet schedules. When you have completed each step, sign off each workprogram step with your initials and the date of completion. An example of the prior year workpapers is also available for your use. This file is called AuditPrior.xls and contains examples of each of the schedules that you will need to complete in the current year.

When you have completed the audit workprogram, print out the workprogram (dated and initialed) and all related worksheets. Best wishes with your first assignment.

Note: The current year workprogram, AuditScheds.xls, and the prior year workprogram, AuditPrior.xls, are available on this book's website. However, you do not need these website files to complete the audit case. You can complete all assignments starting from a blank worksheet. A copy of the AuditScheds worksheets are provided on the following pages.

Listing of Files

File Identification Area:
Name:
Company: Toy Co, Inc.
File: AuditScheds.xls
Worksheet : list of files
Title: Listing of Files
Date: Audit for Year Ended 20x3

Input/Output Area
Current Year Workpapers

Worksheet Name	Description
list of files	list of worksheets in the workbook file
workprogram	listing of workprogram steps to complete
pbc	prepared by client materials
cash paid interest	worksheet to calculate cash paid for interest
prepaid insurance	calculation of prepaid insurance
depreciation expense	reasonableness test of depreciation expense
operating leases	calculation of operating lease rent expense

Audit Workprogram Steps

File Identification Area:
Name:
Company: Toy Co, Inc.
File: AuditScheds.xls
Worksheet : workprogram
Title: Audit Workprogram Steps
Date: Audit for Year Ended 20x3

Input/Output Area

Audit Procedure   **Initial & Date**

1. Prepare the Cash Paid for Interest disclosure for the Cash Flow Statement.
    a. List the prior accrued interest account. This is interest
that was expensed in the prior year, but not paid until this year.
    b. Add to the above amount the total interest expense booked by
the company for the year ended 20x3.
    c. Subtract the current year accrued interest account balance
from the above total. This is interest that has been expensed
in the current year, but has not yet been paid.
    d. Show the amount of cash paid for interest that should be
disclosed in the financials and sign off all work program steps.
2. Prepare a schedule and test the balance in the Prepaid Insurance Account.
    a. List each insurance policy name, the dates that the policy covers
and the amount of each policy.
    b. Based on the dates of each policy compute the number of months
the policy relates to 20x3.
    c. Based on the price of the policy compute the amount of the policy
related to 20x3. To do this, multiply the months the policy relates to
in 20x3 divided by the total months of the policy times the price
of the policy for that period.
    d. Based on the payment dates given by the company,
compute the amount of cash paid on the insurance policy in 20x3.
(Note that you should only include the amounts paid during the current
policy-do not include amounts the company would have paid on the
previous policy term that would have been paid in 20x3)
    e. Determine the amount of the prepaid expenses for insurance by
subtracting the amount of expense related to 20x3 from the amount
of expense actually paid in 20x3.
    f. Sum the total of the prepaid for each of the policies.
    g. Compare the computed total prepaid based on the policies
to the amount in the general ledger.

Audit Workprogram Steps (continued)

h. Conclude about the adequacy of the prepaid insurance balance. Assume that amounts should be investigated further unless the differences are truly immaterial. (Immaterial amounts are those less than $5,000 for this client.)

3. Prepare a reasonableness test of depreciation expense.
   a. Record the opening and closing account balance for each of the individual property accounts.
   b. Using the opening and closing property balances, compute the average account balance by adding the beginning and ending amounts and dividing by two.
   c. Record the useful life of each asset class.
   d. Divide the average account balance during the year by the useful life of the asset to compute estimated depreciation expense.
   e. Record the actual depreciation expense for each asset classification.
   f. Compare each asset class to the estimated depreciation. Also compare the overall totals for all of the depreciable assets. List any accounts that you feel have differences that should be further evaluated.

4. Prepare a schedule of and test rent expense.
   a. List each of the lease names for the operating leases, the annual amount of the lease, and the number of months that the lease was held by the company.
   b. Compute monthly expense by dividing the annual rents by 12.
   c. Determine the estimated rental amounts by multiplying the monthly rate computed in part b by the number of months the lease was held by the company.
   d. Add the rents for each of the leases and compare the total to the total in the rental expense account per the general ledger.
   e. Conclude about the reasonableness of the rent expense accounts. Discuss here if you would need to do additional procedures.

Information Prepared by Client

File Identification Area:
Name:
Company: Toy Co, Inc.
File: AuditScheds.xls
Worksheet : pbc
Title: Information Prepared by Client
Date: Audit for Year Ended 20x3

Input/Output Area

α	ties to general ledger
β	ties to prior year
χ	agreed to lease agreement terms
δ	agrees to insurance policy terms & invoices
ε	agrees to company policy for depreciable asset class

Account Balances:

Account Name	*Balance*	
Prior Year 12/31/x2		
Accrued Interest	$ 1,985	β
Building	$ 1,548,958	β
Office Furniture & Equipment	$ 495,255	β
Automobiles	$ 45,966	β
Machinery & Factory Equipment	$ 3,568,741	β
Computers and Software	$ 158,624	β
Semi-Trucks	$ 5,321,427	β
Current Year 12/31/x3		
Balance Sheet		
Accrued Interest	$ 2,564	α
Prepaid Insurance	$ 14,789	α
Building	$ 1,548,958	α
Office Furniture & Equipment	$ 486,585	α
Automobiles	$ 70,213	α
Machinery & Factory Equipment	$ 4,526,584	α
Computers and Software	$ 167,525	α
Semi-Trucks	$ 5,587,895	α

Information Prepared by Client (continued)

Income Statement

Interest Expense	$	23,856 α
Building Depreciation Expense	$	51,632 α
Office Furniture & Equipment Depreciation Expense	$	51,485 α
Automobiles Depreciation Expense	$	10,253 α
Machinery & Factory Equipment Depreciation Expense	$	499,524 α
Computers and Software Depreciation Expense	$	54,351 α
Semi-Trucks Depreciation Expense	$	505,428 α
Rent Expense	$	42,925 α

Insurance Information

Type	Term	Payments		Cost	
Directors & Officers	7/1/x3-6/30/x4	$ 4,000	$	4,000	δ
Property Insurance	5/1/x3-4/30/x4	$ 45,000	$	60,000	δ
Auto Insurance	1/1/x3-12/31/x3	$ 7,000	$	7,000	δ
Workers Compensation	10/1/x3-9/30/x4	$ 15,000	$	30,000	δ

Depreciable Life Information

Asset	Useful Life
Building	30 ε
Office Furniture & Equipment	10 ε
Automobiles	5 ε
Machinery & Factory Equipment	7 ε
Computers and Software	3 ε
Semi-Trucks	12 ε

Lease Information

Lease	Start Date	End Date	Yearly Rentals	
Mail Machine (Postage)	1/1/x3	12/31/x3	$ 450	χ
Copier XL34	5/1/x2	4/30/x5	$ 1,500	χ
Warehouse Space	1/1/x3	12/31/x3	$ 32,000	χ
Copier XL25	1/1/x1	12/31/x3	$ 1,300	χ
Copier XZ17	7/1/x3	6/30/x6	$ 1,850	χ
Corporate Apartment	10/1/x0	9/30/x3	$ 9,000	χ

PRIOR YEAR WORKPAPERS

File Identification Area:
Name:
Company: Toy Co, Inc.
File: AuditPrior.xls
Worksheet : cash paid interest
Title: Cash Paid for Interest Computation
Date: Audit for Year Ended 20x2

Input Area:

Accrued Interest at December 31, 20x1	$ 2,548
Interest Expense for the Year Ended 20x2	$ 34,855
Accrued Interest at December 31, 20x2	$ 1,985

Output Area:

Accrued Interest at December 31, 20x1	$ 2,548
Interest Expense for the Year Ended 20x2	$ 34,855
Accrued Interest at December 31, 20x2	$ (1,985)
Cash Paid for Interest 20x2	$ 35,418

File Identification Area:
Name:
Company: Toy Co, Inc.
File: AuditPrior.xls
Worksheet : prepaid insurance
Title: Prepaid Insurance Calculation
Date: Audit for Year Ended 20x2

Input Area:

Name of Insurace	Policy Term	Amount of Policy	Months in 20x2	Months in Policy	Payments in 20x2*
Directors & Officers	7/1/x2-6/30/x3	$ 3,500	6	12	$ 3,500
Property Insurance	5/1/x2-4/30/x3	$ 48,000	8	12	$ 36,000
Auto Insurance	1/1/x2-12/31/x2	$ 6,500	12	12	$ 6,500
Workers Comp.	10/1/x2-9/30/x3	$ 24,000	3	12	$ 12,000

Current Year Prepaid Per General Ledger $ 11,758

Ouput Area:

Name of Insurace	Policy Term	Amount of Policy	Months in 20x2	Months in Policy	Expense in 20x2	Payments in 20x2*	Payments in excess of expense
Directors & Officers	7/1/x2-6/30/x3	$ 3,500	6	12	$ 1,750	$ 3,500	$ 1,750
Property Insurance	5/1/x2-4/30/x3	$ 48,000	8	12	$ 32,000	$ 36,000	$ 4,000
Auto Insurance	1/1/x2-12/31/x2	$ 6,500	12	12	$ 6,500	$ 6,500	$ -
Workers Comp.	10/1/x2-9/30/x3	$ 24,000	3	12	$ 6,000	$ 12,000	$ 6,000

Total x2 prepaid $ 11,750

Amount per General Ledger $ 11,758

Difference from General Ledger $ (8)

* Includes only payments related to current policy. Payments made during the year for the prior year policy are not included.

File Identification Area:
Name:
Company: Toy Co, Inc.
File: AuditPrior.xls
Worksheet : depreciation expense
Title: Reasonableness Test of Depreciation
Date: Audit for Year Ended 20x2

Input Area:

Account Name	12/31/x1	12/31/x2	Useful life of Asset Class	Actual Expense for 20x2
Building	$ 1,548,958	$ 1,548,958	30	$ 51,632
Office Furniture & Fixtures	$ 490,255	$ 495,255	10	$ 48,853
Automobiles	$ 30,301	$ 45,966	5	$ 7,786
Machinery & Factory Equipment	$ 3,159,564	$ 3,568,741	7	$ 485,630
Computers & Software	$ 160,555	$ 158,624	3	$ 51,254
Semi-Trucks	$ 5,119,545	$ 5,321,427	12	$ 430,850

Output Area:

Account Name	12/31/x1	12/31/x2	Average balance for 20x2	Useful life of Asset Class	Estimated Expense for 20x2	Actual Expense for 20x2	Difference: Actual to Estimated
Building	$ 1,548,958	$ 1,548,958	$ 1,548,958	30	$ 51,632	$ 51,632	$ (0)
Office Furniture & Fixtures	$ 490,255	$ 495,255	$ 492,755	10	$ 49,276	$ 48,853	$ 423
Automobiles	$ 30,301	$ 45,966	$ 38,134	5	$ 7,627	$ 7,786	$ (159)
Machinery & Factory Equipment	$ 3,159,564	$ 3,568,741	$ 3,364,153	7	$ 480,593	$ 485,630	$ (5,037)
Computers & Software	$ 160,555	$ 158,624	$ 159,590	3	$ 53,197	$ 51,254	$ 1,943
Semi-Trucks	$ 5,119,545	$ 5,321,427	$ 5,220,486	12	$ 435,041	$ 430,850	$ 4,191
				Totals	$ 1,077,364	$1,076,005	$ 1,359

File Identification Area:
Name:
Company: Toy Co, Inc.
File: AuditPrior.xls
Worksheet : operating leases
Title: Operating Leases Schedule
Date: Audit for Year Ended 20x2

Input Area:

	Yearly Lease Amount		Months Leased in 20x2
Mail machine	$	425	12
Copier XL34	$	1,500	8
Warehouse Space	$	30,000	12
Copier XL25	$	1,300	12
Corporate Apartment	$	9,000	12

Rent Expense Per the General Ledger		$	41,700

Output Area:

	Yearly Lease Amount		Monthly Payment		Months Leased in 20x2	Est. Rent Expense for 20x2	
Mail machine	$	425	$	35	12	$	425
Copier XL34	$	1,500	$	125	8	$	1,000
Warehouse Space	$	30,000	$	2,500	12	$	30,000
Copier XL25	$	1,300	$	108	12	$	1,300
Corporate Apartment	$	9,000	$	750	12	$	9,000
			Total			$	41,725
			Amount per General Ledger			$	41,700
			Difference Est. to G/L			$	25

SOLUTIONS
to
Selected Assignments

1. INCOME STATEMENT

FILE IDENTIFICATION AREA:

Name:
Date Created:
Filename: AA01.xls

INPUT AREA:

Sales: 100,000
Cost of Sales as % of Sales   50%
Operating Expenses   15,000

OUTPUT AREA:

CHRIS RAY'S CARD SHOP
INCOME STATEMENT
FYE 12/31/x1

Sales	$100,000
Cost of Sales	50,000
Gross profit	$50,000
Operating Expenses	15,000
Net income	$35,000
	======

21.   ATTRIBUTE SAMPLING: DETERMINING SAMPLE SIZE

IDENTIFICATION AREA:

Name:
Filename: AA21.xls
Date:

INPUT AREA:

Directions: Use the tables below for attribute sampling.
   1. Table 1: Determine sample size (go to cell A58).
   2. Table 2: Evaluate sample results (go to cell A79).

OUTPUT AREA: Record results here; replace each "?"
                         with appropriate number:

Reliability is set at 95%

ERO =   3 %
TRO =   6 %
Thus, sample size is: 200

23.   ATTRIBUTE SAMPLING: EVALUATING RESULTS

IDENTIFICATION AREA:

Name:
Filename: AA23.xls
Date:

INPUT AREA:

Directions: Use the tables below for attribute sampling.

　1. Table 1: Determine sample size (go to cell A58).

　2. Table 2: Evaluate sample results (go to cell A79).

OUTPUT AREA: Record results here; replace each "?"
                          with appropriate number:

Reliability is set at 95%

ERO =   ?   %

TRO =   8 %

Thus, sample size is: 300

Occurrences (errors) =   25

UPL =   12 %

UPL > TRO; thus, the auditor cannot rely upon the control.

25.   VARIABLES SAMPLING: DETERMINING SAMPLE SIZE

FILE IDENTIFICATION AREA:

Name:
Filename: AA25.xls
Date Created:

INPUT AREA:

Directions:

Part 1: Determine sample size for variables sampling plan.
              Go to cell A85.

Part 2: Evaluate sample results.
              Go to cell A106.

INPUT/OUTPUT - PART 1: DETERMINE SAMPLE SIZE

Formulas:

$A = TE * R(IR)/[R(IR)+R(IA)]$

$n = [(N * R(IR) * SD)/A]^2$

To compute n, enter values for TE, R(IR), R(IA), N, and SD:

	AA25
TE	100,000
R(IR)	1.65
R(IA)	1.65
N	1,000
SD	300
A	50,000
Sample size (n)	98

29.   VARIABLES SAMPLING: EVALUATING RESULTS

FILE IDENTIFICATION AREA:

Filename: AA29.xls

Date Created:

INPUT AREA:

Directions: Part 1: Determine sample size for variables sampling plan.

Go to cell A85.

Part 2: Evaluate sample results.

Go to cell A106.

INPUT/OUTPUT - PART 2: EVALUATE SAMPLE RESULTS

To compute Prec, enter values for N, R(IR), sd, and n:

	Situations:
	AA29

N	1000
R(IR)	1.65
sd	9
n	81
Prec =	1650

Formula: Prec=N*R(IR)*(sd/(@sqrt(n)))

Enter sample mean and client's book value (BV):

	Situations:
	AA29

Sample mean =	999
EAV=	999,000
Client's BV =	1,000,000
Lower DI value =	997,350
Upper DI value =	1,000,650
Auditor Decision:	Accept

35.   COST-VOLUME-PROFIT ANALYSIS

FILE IDENTIFICATION AREA:
Name:
Date Created:
Filename: AA35.xls

INPUT AREA:

Sales Price Per Item	=	$10.00
Variable Cost Per Item	=	$8.00
Total Fixed Cost	=	$24,000

OUTPUT AREA:

Sales Price	$10.00
Variable Cost	8.00
Contribution Margin	$2.00
Fixed Cost	$24,000
Breakeven Point in Units	12,000
Breakeven Point in Dollars	$120,000

49.   BUDGETED COSTS: ABC COST PER UNIT   (Page 1 of 2)

FILE IDENTIFICATION AREA:
Name:
Filename: AA49.xls
Date Created:

INPUT AREA:

Materials handling allocation rate	$1.25
Machine setups allocation rate	$300.00
Insertion of parts allocation rate	$3.00
Finishing allocation rate	$70.00

OUTPUT AREA:
A.

Chromex
Total Budgeted Indirect Costs

Activity	Budgeted Quantity of cost Allocation Base		Cost Allocation Rate	Total Budgeted Indirect Cost
Materials handling	12,000	*	$1.25	15,000
Machine setups	6	**	$300.00	1,800
Insertion of parts	12,000	*	$3.00	36,000
Finishing	1,200	***	$70.00	84,000
Total budgeted ABC costs				136,800
				========

* (5*1000) + (7*1000)
** 3+3
*** (.2*1000) + (1*1000)

49. BUDGETED COSTS: ABC COST PER UNIT (Page 2 of 2)

OUTPUT AREA CONTINUED:

B.

Chromex
ABC Costs per Unit

Activity	Cost Allocation Rate	Quantity of Cost Allocation Base Used By:		Allocated Activity Cost per Wheel	
		Standard	Deluxe	Standard	Deluxe
Materials handling	$1.25	5	7	6.25	8.75
Machine setups	$300.00	0.003 *	0.003	0.90	0.90
Insertion of parts	$3.00	5	7	15.00	21.00
Finishing	$70.00	0.2	1	14.00	70.00
ABC Costs per Unit				$36.15	$100.65
				========	=======

* 3 setups/1000 wheels = .003 per wheel

C.

Budgeted total ABC manufacturing cost (Req. A above) = $136,800

Budgeted total direct labor hours = (1000*2) + (1000*3)
=   2,000 + 3,000
=   5,000

Single allocation rate = Total Budgeted Cost / Total Direct Labor Hours
Single allocation rate   = $136,800 /   5,000   = $27.36 per direct labor hour

Indirect manufacturing cost per wheel:

Standard model:	2 *	$27.36	=	$54.72
Deluxe model:	3 *	$27.36	=	$82.08

61. FOREIGN CURRENCY TRANSLATION USING THE CURRENT RATE METHOD (Page 1 of 2)

FILE IDENTIFICATION AREA:

Name:

Filename: AA61.xls

Date Created:

INPUT AREA:

ADJUSTED TRIAL BALANCE
In Dutch Guilders (DG)
December 31, Year 4

	Debit	Credit
Cash	20,000	
Accounts Receivable	35,000	
Inventory	105,000	
Equipment	60,000	
Accum. Dep.		20,000
Accounts Payable		35,000
Bonds Payable		50,000
Revenues		120,000
General Expenses	108,000	
Depreciation Expense	8,000	
Dividends	4,000	
Common Stock		62,000
Paid-in Capital in Excess of Par		44,000
Retained Earnings		9,000
Total	340,000	340,000

Exchange Rates:

	1 DG = $___
Current Exchange Rate	0.520
Average Exchange Rate	0.490
At July 31, Year 4	0.505
At June 30, Year 1	0.470

Other: All common stock was issued on June 30, Year 1 (i.e., 6/30/Y1).

Dividends were declared and paid on July 31, Year 4.

Translated Retained Earnings at 12/31/Y4 was: $5,500

61.   FOREIGN CURRENCY TRANSLATION USING THE CURRENT RATE METHOD   (Page 2 of 2)

OUTPUT AREA:

TRANSLATION FROM DUTCH GUILDERS TO DOLLARS
CURRENT RATE METHOD

Debits:		DG's	Exchange Rates	U.S. $'s
	Cash	20,000	0.520	10,400
	A/R	35,000	0.520	18,200
	Inventory	105,000	0.520	54,600
	Fixed Assets	60,000	0.520	31,200
	General Expenses	108,000	0.490	52,920
	Depreciation Exp.	8,000	0.490	3,920
	Dividends (7/31/Y4)	4,000	0.505	2,020
Total		340,000		173,260
Credits:				
	Accum. Depreciation	20,000	0.520	10,400
	A/P	35,000	0.520	18,200
	Bonds Payable	50,000	0.520	26,000
	Revenues	120,000	0.490	58,800
	Common Stock (6/30/Y1)	62,000	0.470	29,140
	Paid-in Cap. (6/30/Y1)	44,000	0.470	20,680
	Retained Earnings	9,000	n.a.	5,500
	Cum. Transl. Adjustment			4,540
Total		340,000		173,260

Index